102

33.⁰⁰

Oregon

AMERICA THE BEAUTIFUL

second series

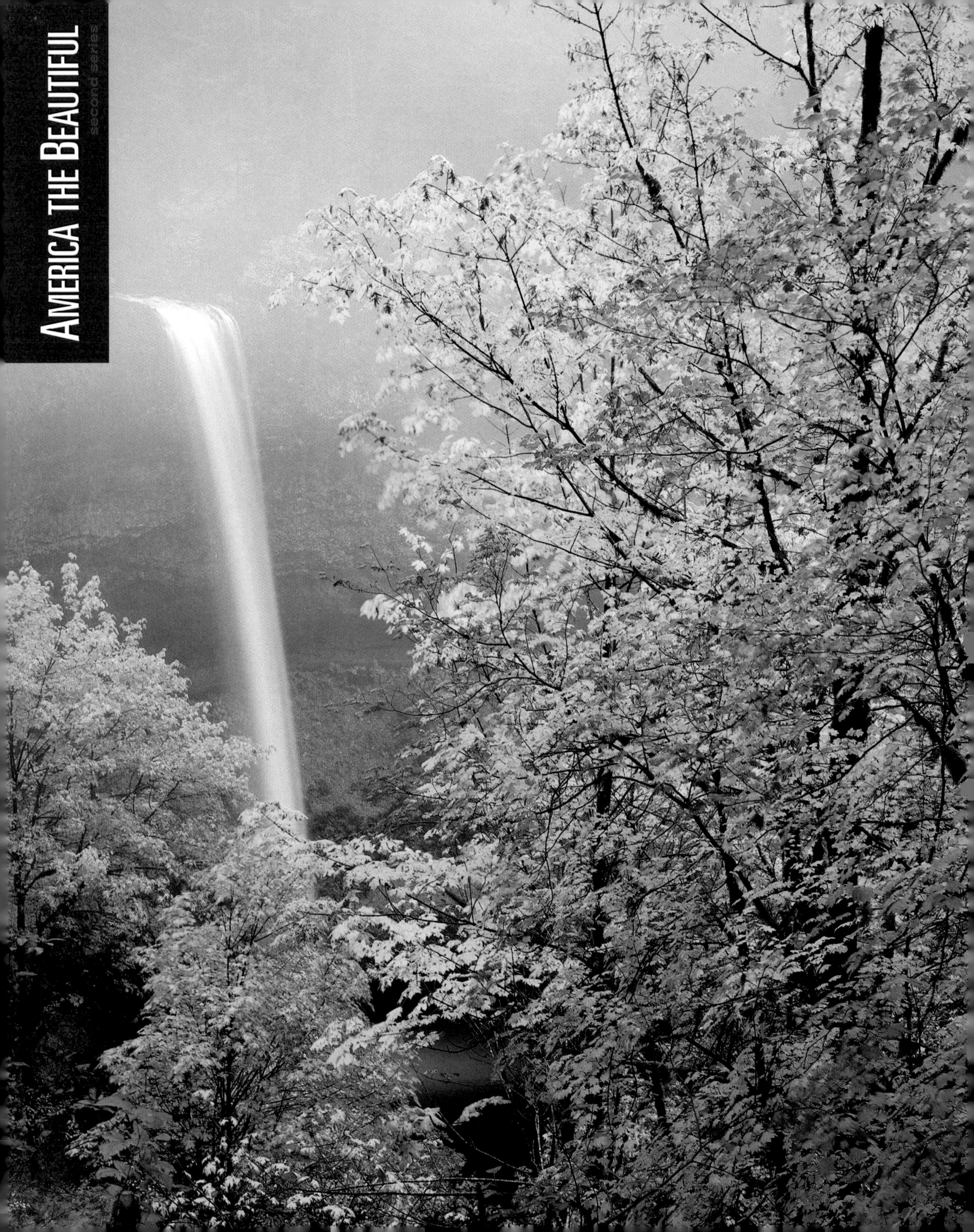

Oregon

W. Scott Ingram

Children's Press®
A Division of Grolier Publishing
New York   London   Hong Kong   Sydney
Danbury, Connecticut

Frontispiece: Bigleaf and fine maples in fall

Front cover: Portland's Washington Park with Mount Hood in the background

Back cover: Heceta Head Lighthouse

Consultant: Craig Smith, Oregon State Library

Please note: All statistics are as up-to-date as possible at the time of publication.

Visit Children's Press on the Internet at http://publishing.grolier.com

Book production by Editorial Directions, Inc.

Library of Congress Cataloging-in-Publication Data

Ingram, Scott (William Scott)
    Oregon / by W. Scott Ingram.
      144 p. 24 cm. — (America the beautiful. Second series)
    Includes bibliographical references and index.
    Summary : Describes the geography, plants, animals, history, economy, language, religions, culture, sports, arts, and people of Oregon.
    ISBN 0-516-20996-5
    1. Oregon—Juvenile literature. [1. Oregon.] I. Title. II. Series.
    F876.3.I64 2000   99-20967
    979.521—dc21

Acknowledgments

The author would like to express sincere gratitude to the people of Oregon who have created the wealth of research materials about their state. In particular, the information provided by the End of the Oregon Trail Interpretive Center helped to bring the past alive. I would also like to thank my son, Miles, whose valuable research skills were much appreciated.

Mount Hood

Grazing sheep

Douglas firs

Contents

The spotted owl

Smith Rock

Eugene

A Portland powwow

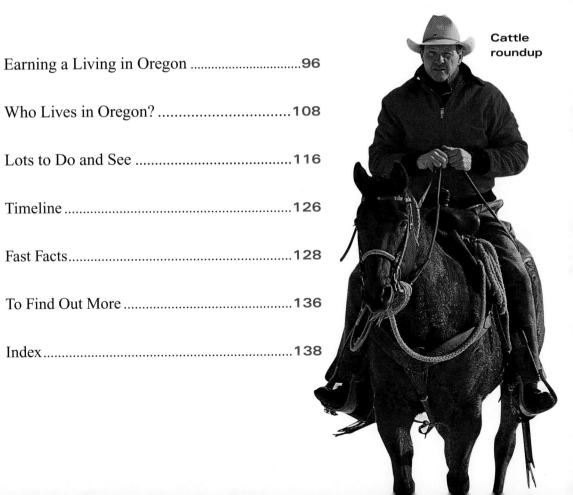
Cattle roundup

CHAPTER ONE

A Parade of History

People have been coming to the Big Wagon Days festival since the End of the Oregon Trail Interpretive Center opened in 1995. Traveling down the Willamette Valley in oxen-drawn wagons, they feel just like their great-great-grandparents did when they arrived in the 1850s. For many, Big Wagon Days every August is a family tradition.

Of course these modern-day travelers have it a lot easier than the real pioneers did. They travel for only a few days along good roads and bridges and stay at motels or campgrounds. Back in the 1850s, people on the Oregon Trail had it a lot harder. Many of them never even made it all the way to Oregon City.

It is hard to imagine walking 2,000 miles (3,200 kilometers) across the country from Independence, Missouri, to Oregon City. The prairie schooners—that's what covered wagons were called back then—didn't have springs. Their wheels were made of hardwood with iron rims. And there were no rubber tires or paved

This covered wagon is on display at the End of the Oregon Trail Interpretive Center.

Opposite: The End of the Oregon Trail Interpretive Center in Oregon City

Traveling on the Oregon Trail

roads. Anyone who rode in a prairie schooner would bounce around like a jumping bean. Women back then would fill butter churns with fresh milk in the morning, and after a day of bouncing in the wagon, there would be butter in the churn.

Traveling on the trail was no vacation. Accidents happened all the time. Sometimes the bouncing of the wagons caused loaded guns to misfire and hurt people. Little children could be crushed under heavy wagon wheels or drown in rivers. And anyone— young or old—could get sick from eating spoiled food or drinking dirty water. Everyone had to drink the same water that the oxen drank—water that had already been used by other wagon

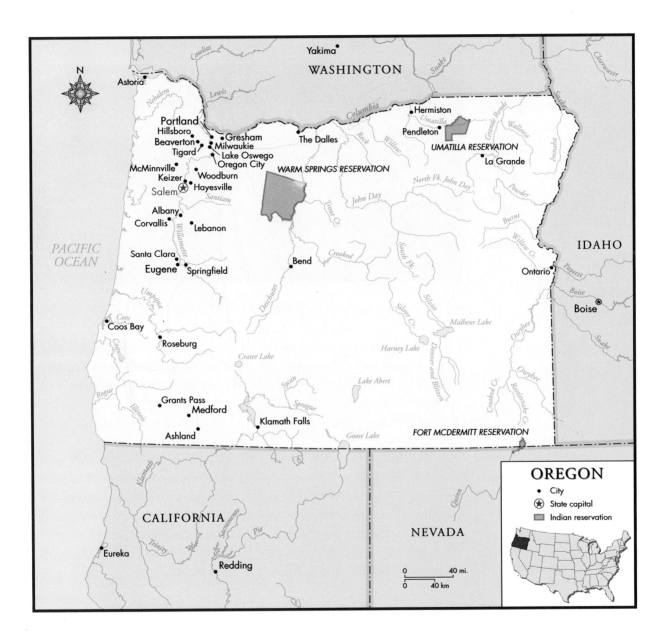

**Geopolitical map
of Oregon**

The End of the Trail

For most weary travelers in the 1840s and 1850s, the end of the Oregon Trail was Oregon City on the Willamette River (above). Oregon City was then the capital of the territory. The first provisional governor, elected in 1845, was a local merchant named George Abernethy. Abernethy wanted to see the region prosper, so he allowed newly arrived travelers to park their wagons, graze their animals, and set up camp in a meadow behind his house.

That meadow came to be known as Abernethy Green, and word traveled back east that this beautiful field was the true end of the trail.

In 1995, the End of the Oregon Trail Interpretive Center was opened on the site of what was once Abernethy Green. The center's wagon-shaped buildings include a museum, a library, and several theaters that tell visitors about the rich history of Oregon country. ▮

trains—and had to camp among the garbage left by wagon trains that had gone before.

Everyone traveling on the Oregon Trail had to work hard. Children gathered wood or animal droppings for cooking fires.

They also fed and watered the oxen and other livestock. Older boys went a short distance ahead of the wagons to fish or gather wild berries for food.

Hunting, repairing broken wagons, trading with Native Americans—those were jobs for the men. The women cooked, washed, mended, and cared for the sick or injured. And everyone walked, except babies and the weakest people. One step after another, mile after mile, for five months or more in rain and heat, they walked across prairies, mountains, rivers, and deserts until they reached Oregon.

Anyone who walked that far had to be strong. Some people had horses to pull their wagons, even though they weren't as strong as oxen and they got hurt more often. Some people used mules, but they were expensive and hard to train. So most people used oxen. A team of four to six was enough to pull a big wagon. Oxen weren't picky about what they grazed on, and although they walked slowly, they almost always got to Oregon.

Some of the Big Wagon Days parade participants dress in beaver hats and buckskins like fur trappers. Cowboys at the event wear chaps and spurs. And some Native Americans dress in beautiful tribal clothing. Oregon is a living history book—that's what makes life there so interesting.

CHAPTER TWO

Natives, Traders, and Trappers

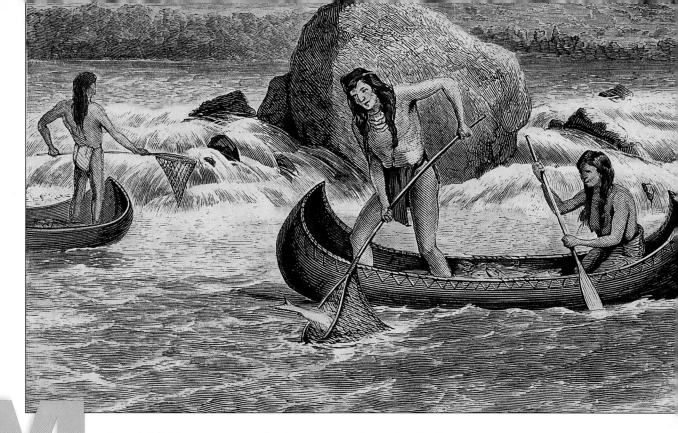

Native Americans
often caught salmon
in the Columbia River.

More than 14,000 years ago, glaciers covered much of what we know today as North America. When the glaciers melted, groups of people made their way across a land bridge from Asia to Alaska and then south to the coast and waterways of the place we now call Oregon. Remains of village sites more than 11,000 years old have been found along the Columbia River. In 1938, archaeologists working in central Oregon found sandals made of sagebrush and bark that were determined to be more than 13,000 years old.

Eventually, these first Native Americans settled in several regions: the coast, the Willamette Valley, and the Columbia Plateau. Before the arrival of white settlers, about one hundred Native American tribes lived in Oregon.

Among the coastal tribes were the Chinook, the Yaquina, and Tututni. In this area of abundant food resources and a mild climate,

Opposite: The first
fur-trading site of John
Jacob Astor in what is
now Oregon

Natives, Traders, and Trappers **15**

the people built permanent villages out of cedar. Coastal groups harvested shellfish and trapped salmon and trout. They hunted waterfowl with bows and arrows.

The eastern slopes of the Cascade Range, in the southern area of the state, were home to the Klamath-Modoc people. In winter, the people lived in earthen shelters, and in summer, they lived in portable tepees. The Klamath-Modoc society had rich families and poor families. The poorest people sometimes served the wealthy as slaves.

The wide, flat lands of the Columbia Plateau were home to the Shoshone, Nez Perce, Walla Walla, and Yakima tribes, among others. The Indians lived in tepees or in tentlike structures called wickiups made of woven mats and brush. They lived on buffalo, deer, roots, plants, and berries. The Nez Perce was the largest Native American group in the plateau and the first to tame and use horses.

First Europeans

Christopher Columbus, John Cabot, Henry Hudson, and many other early European explorers came to North and South America searching for an entirely different place—China. When the Europeans realized that two enormous continents and the vast Pacific Ocean lay before them, another search began. They wanted to find a shorter route connecting the Atlantic and Pacific Oceans.

As more Europeans explored North America, they began to dream of finding a "Northwest Passage," an inland waterway across North America. However, the Northwest Passage was a myth. No European realized how big North America was.

During the sixteenth century, European explorers sailed up the west coast in search of riches, trade routes, and possible sites for colonies. Spanish explorers were the first white men to sail along the Oregon coast, but they did not land. In 1579, the famous English buccaneer Sir Francis Drake reached the Oregon coast at a place called Little Whale Cove, but thick fog along the beaches and inlets prevented him from landing. The enormous size of North America and the difficulty of sailing all the way around the tip of South America to reach the west coast slowed European exploration of the northwest coast. But the search for a shorter route between the Atlantic and Pacific continued.

Sir Francis Drake

In 1775, as the American Revolution was beginning on the other side of the continent, a Spanish explorer named Bruno Heceta sailed to the mouth of what he described as "a great river or some passage to another sea." In 1778, English explorer Captain James Cook reached this same "great river." Instead of exploring the river, however, Cook traded with the natives for the furs of sea otter and beaver. Continuing across the Pacific toward China, Cook intended to sell the furs for a fortune.

In 1792, an American trader named Captain Robert Gray became the first white person to set foot in Oregon. Gray sailed up

Captain Robert Gray

the great river that he named for his ship, the *Columbia*. As the eighteenth century came to a close, the United States, Russia, England, and Spain had all laid claim to the land of the Chinook, the Klamath-Modoc, the Shoshone, and other Native American groups. And many explorers still believed that the great river led all the way to the Atlantic Ocean.

Trade with China paved the way for Europeans to come to Oregon. Soon Russian and French explorers had made their way to the northwest coast in search of furs.

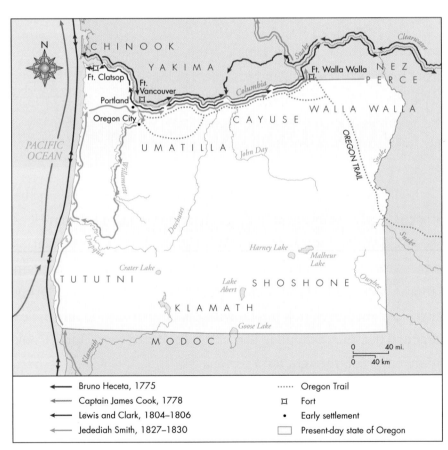

Exploration of Oregon

Name Origins

The name *Oregon* is believed to have come from the French word *ouragan*, meaning "storm" or "hurricane," but many other names and terms came from the Native American tribes that lived in the Northwest. Tribal names are reflected today in chinook salmon, the Klamath Mountains, and towns such as Tillamook.

European explorers have also given their names to Oregon places. Heceta Head is named for the first Spanish explorer to sail along the coast past the mouth of the Columbia. Astoria is named for John Jacob Astor (left), an American businessman who built a fort at the mouth of the Columbia River as a fur-trading outpost.

The name of one famous Northwest Native American tribe comes from French instead of the tribe's own language. In 1805, the Lewis and Clark expedition met natives in Oregon who called themselves *Nee-Mee-Poo*, meaning "the people" in their language. A French trapper who spoke Indian languages was traveling with the expedition as a translator. He mispronounced the name of the tribe as *Nez Perce*, the French term for "pierced nose." Although "the people" did not pierce their noses, as some coastal tribes did, the name stuck. ■

Lewis and Clark

Soon after Thomas Jefferson became president in 1801, the United States acquired a vast territory west of the Mississippi River, extending from the Gulf of Mexico to the Rocky Mountains. For more than two centuries, the area had been under either Spanish or French control and was named *Louisiana*, after King Louis XIV of France. The French emperor Napoleon needed money for his war in Europe. Thus, France sold this region to the United States. The transaction, known as the Louisiana Purchase, doubled the size of the country.

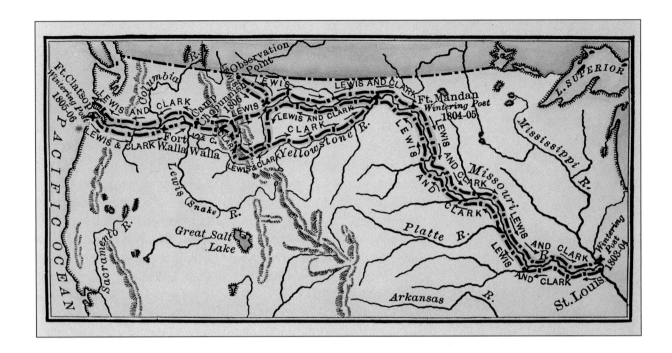

A map of the Lewis and Clark expedition

Jefferson wanted Americans to explore the Louisiana Territory to determine whether the Missouri River was connected to the Columbia. Such a connection would form an inland waterway across the country and give the United States a Northwest Passage—and enormous power in the fur trade.

In 1804, with Jefferson's support, Captain Meriwether Lewis and Lieutenant William Clark set out with a group of forty-five hardy men to explore the Louisiana Territory. Their journey took them from the trading post of St. Louis up the Missouri River to the Rocky Mountains and across the rugged Northwest. A young Shoshone woman named Sacajawea aided them greatly in their travels.

In October 1805, the party reached the Columbia River. Because it was too late in the year to return, Lewis and Clark

Sacajawea (above) is one of the most interesting and mysterious women in the story of America's westward expansion. Even the spelling of her name is a mysterious; sometimes it is spelled *Sacagawea*. The Shoshone people, whose tribal lands were in the Oregon Territory, spell her name with a *j*. In his journal, Clark refers to the young Native American woman as "Bird Woman," the English translation of her Indian name.

Bird Woman

It is believed that Sacajawea was born in 1789 to a Shoshone family in what is now Idaho. At age ten, she was captured in a raid by the Hidatsa tribe and taken to present-day North Dakota. When she was fifteen, Sacajawea was sold to a French-Canadian fur trader, Toussaint Charbonneau. Lewis and Clark met the two when their party spent the winter of 1804–1805 in a Hidatsa village. During those months, Sacajawea, sixteen, gave birth to a son who was named Jean Baptiste.

At winter's end, Charbonneau, who knew the area well, was hired as a guide and told to bring his wife and infant on the journey. Clark felt that traveling with a woman and baby would show any Indians they encountered that they traveled in peace. Sacajawea also knew several languages and understood the customs of the tribes in the huge territory.

Sacajawea's knowledge of the territory saved the party weeks of travel. She was also able to barter for horses and supplies with Native Americans along the way. When food was scarce, she gathered roots, nuts, and berries to feed the expedition. Lewis and Clark named Lake Sacajawea in Idaho in her honor.

Sacajawea, Jean Baptiste, and Charbonneau accompanied Lewis and Clark to the mouth of the Columbia and spent the rainy winter of 1805–1806 in Fort Clatsop. Charbonneau had become physically abusive during the journey. Clark, concerned for the welfare of the young woman and her baby, offered to take Jean Baptiste back with him to St. Louis and raise him as his son.

On the return trip, however, the three returned to the Hidatsa village where they had met Lewis and Clark. Little is known of the rest of Sacajawea's life. Records show that she did go to St. Louis and allow Clark to raise Jean Baptiste. What happened to her after that is uncertain. Clark's records claim she died of smallpox at the age of twenty-five. Shoshone history, however, claims that she married several times, had many children, and lived in Wyoming to the age of ninety-six. ■

Winter at Fort Clatsop

In late 1805, Lewis and Clark had hoped that they might find a trading ship at the mouth of the Columbia River to take them back home. But, as winter fog and storms arrived, the party was forced to build shelter and wait out the rainy months. In December, they erected a log stockade 50 by 50 feet (15 by 15 m). Inside the walls were two rows of rooms separated by a parade ground. They called the stockade Fort Clatsop.

The men spent their days boiling seawater to extract the salt they needed to preserve meat for the return trip. They lived on boiled elk meat, using the animals' skins to make clothing to replace clothes that had rotted during the journey. Relations with the nearby natives were mostly peaceful, but the constant rain made everyone short-tempered. From early December until late March, the sun came out on only six days! Clark wrote these words in his famous journal: "O! How disagreeable is our situation during this dreadful weather." Today, Fort Clatsop is a national memorial. ◼

remained in Oregon for the winter of 1805–1806. By the fall of 1806, the Lewis and Clark party had made it back to their starting point—St. Louis, Missouri. From there, word spread quickly about the great natural resources of the Northwest—especially the furs.

Fur Trade and Settlement

The return of Lewis and Clark increased interest in the Northwest. Although the party had not found the Northwest Passage, the knowledge that this vast country was open for fur trapping and trading drew many people across the rugged continent. Fur traders from England and Canada came as well. Most of the traders were after the pelt of one animal in particular—the beaver.

In the early nineteenth century, beaver hats were popular among Americans and Europeans. Beavers had once been abundant in the eastern United States, but the increase in and spread of settlers there had almost wiped them out.

News of so many furs in the Northwest drew trappers and traders from all over. Most followed the route marked by the Lewis and Clark expedition only a few years earlier. Like Lewis and Clark, the adventurers faced obstacles as they paddled up the Missouri River. Broken tree stumps beneath muddy,

Fur trappers came to the Northwest from all parts of the country.

swirling waters tore their canoes apart. Driftwood blocked their way. Thunderstorms, hail, and clouds of mosquitoes made the long trip tortuous.

The lure of fur drew investors too. In 1810, John Jacob Astor, a wealthy businessman, formed his own fur-trading company—the Pacific Fur Company. Astor planned to set up trading posts from the Mississippi River at St. Louis all the way up the Missouri River and then west to the Pacific Ocean. On the Columbia River, Astor planned to build an outpost that could serve as a depot to carry furs and other goods across the Pacific. In 1811, the town of Astoria was built at the mouth of the Columbia.

Events did not go smoothly at the new settlement. During a trading expedition along the coast of present-day Washington, a ship sailing from Astoria was attacked by Native Americans. Twenty-seven men were killed, and the ship was destroyed in the attack.

Astoria as it appeared in 1813

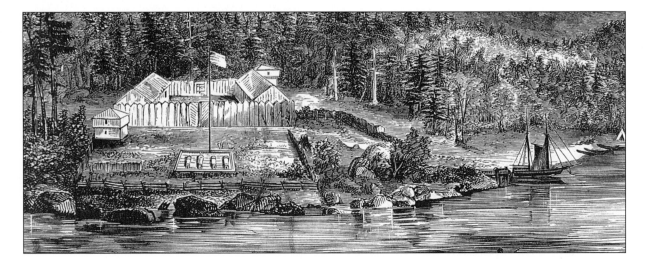

Events in the East also worked against the Astorians. In 1812, war broke out between the United States and England. The fur trade had drawn many men loyal to the English side into the Oregon country. A British warship arrived in 1813 and captured Astoria, renaming it Fort George. Until the war ended in 1815, the British controlled the Oregon country and the fur trade.

The Treaty of Ghent, ending the War of 1812, stated that both countries had to return territory captured during the fighting. The United States laid claim to Astoria as well as the rest of the Oregon country, saying Robert Gray had discovered its main river and Lewis and Clark had explored the area.

The British did not want to give up their hold in Oregon, which then included today's Idaho and Washington as well. In 1818, it was agreed that citizens of both countries could live in Oregon to conduct trade for the following ten years. The agreement was renewed in 1828 and continued until 1846.

At the time of the 1818 agreement, most trappers and traders in Oregon were British or Canadian and almost all worked for the largest fur company in the world—the Hudson's Bay Company. In an effort to keep out American trappers, the owners of the Hudson's Bay Company ordered their men to trap as many beaver as possible. They wanted to wipe out competition by wiping out the animal.

During the 1820s and 1830s, trappers explored southern Oregon and parts of Nevada and California in the never-ending search for furs. Fort Vancouver, established by British traders on the north side of Columbia River, became the main trading post in the wilderness.

A Rugged Life

The life of a trapper, known as a mountain man in the early 1800s, was one of constant danger and hardship. At dawn and sunset, trappers waded into icy streams to place beaver traps in the water. Blazing sun, blizzards, hostile Native Americans, and grizzly bears were daily hazards. Thirst-crazed men sometimes drank animal blood, and starving men might be forced to eat beaver skin, moccasins, crickets, or tree bark.

Trappers who were bitten by rattlesnakes burned gunpowder into the bite to draw out the poison. Trapper Thomas Smith amputated his own leg below the knee when it was shattered in a fall. He soon became known as Pegleg Smith. Famous mountain man Jim Bridger carried an iron arrowhead in his back for years until a missionary cut it out without any anesthetic.

Except for their June rendezvous, mountain men spent most of their time in the wilderness. Preparing for a journey meant stocking up on supplies. Osborne Russell, a trapper who set off on a three-month trip to the eastern Columbia Plateau in 1834, purchased the following:

3 pints flour
2 pints coffee
1/3 pint black pepper
1 blanket
1 knife
1 pair moccasins

1 lb. beads for trade
1/2 lb. gunpowder for trade
1 lb. musket balls for trade

Like most trappers, Russell lived on the buffalo, bear, rabbit, or deer he killed. His only seasoning would be the pepper he carried or salt from mineral springs. He had only one cup of coffee every morning. He used flour to make a special treat called "mountain bread." One explorer wrote: "Our dinner consisted of dry buffalo meat, roots, and fried bread, which was a luxury. Mountain bread is flour mixed with water and fried in buffalo grease. To one who has had nothing but meat for a long time this [tastes] very good." ■

Each summer, trappers brought all the pelts they had gathered to Fort Vancouver. This huge gathering of traders, trappers, and Native Americans was known by the French word for meeting— *rendezvous*. At the yearly rendezvous, merchants bought the furs and shipped them to Europe.

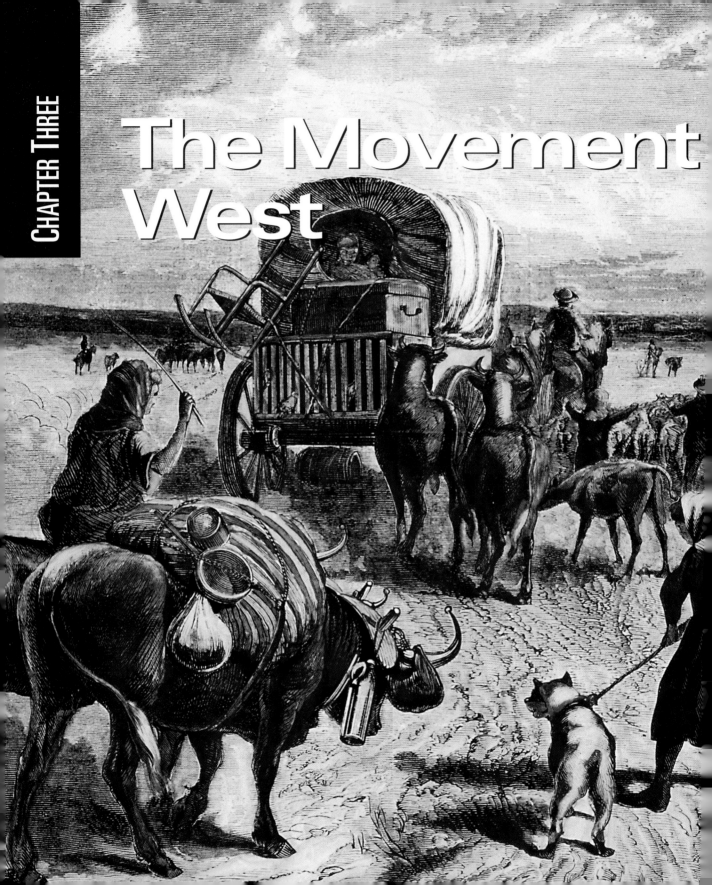

CHAPTER THREE

The Movement West

Fort Vancouver in 1824

Eventually, the British forces who had taken over the American settlement at Astoria abandoned it. Farther up the Columbia River, the British built the outpost called Fort Vancouver. The man in charge of Fort Vancouver was Dr. John McLoughlin, who was also a director of the Hudson's Bay Company.

The first American to reach Oregon overland after the British abandoned Astoria was trapper Jedediah Smith. Traveling north from California in 1828 with a load of furs, Smith passed through the fertile valley of the Willamette River, which flows north into the Columbia. Smith and his party were ambushed by Indians there and robbed of their furs. Several of his companions were killed, but Smith survived and made his way to Fort Vancouver.

Smith was astonished at the size of the British settlement run by the Hudson's Bay Company. A huge square stockade more than 300 feet (91 m) on each side protected warehouses, stores, and offices, and housed more than 400 people. There were fields of crops, herds of livestock, and orchards nearby.

McLoughlin had established good relations with the Indians in the area. Because of this, he was able to recover Smith's stolen furs. But once Smith had sold his furs at the fort, he had to agree to leave Oregon.

Opposite: Heading west in a covered wagon

Settlers from Boston

By the 1830s, the days of trapping and fur trading were drawing to a close everywhere in North America. The beaver population had been almost wiped out, and hats from Chinese silk were now more fashionable than those of beaver.

While the fur trade declined, the young United States grew. Most states east of the Mississippi had been settled, and adventurous Americans continued to push westward across land that they saw as theirs for the taking.

In 1829, a movement called the American Society for Encouraging the Settlement of Oregon Territory began in Boston, Massachusetts. Hall Kelley, the founder of the group, had read about Oregon in the journals of Lewis and Clark. In Oregon country, Kelley believed, the new United States could reach its full potential not by trading furs, but by farming, fishing, and whaling. Kelley and another Bostonian, Nathaniel Wyeth, raised money and bought supplies to lead a party of settlers to Oregon.

Missionaries

At about the same time, a newspaper article appeared throughout the East claiming that American Indians in Oregon wanted to become Christians. Whether or not the article was completely true, two Protestant missionaries, Jason Lee and his nephew, Daniel Lee, decided to go to Oregon to convert Indians to Christianity. In 1834, they joined the group led by Wyeth and Kelley and headed west.

Meanwhile, back in Fort Vancouver, McLoughlin was con-

Salem, the future capital of Oregon, in 1858

cerned because the fur trade was declining. Also, if too many Americans came to Oregon, the British might have to leave.

Hoping to keep any remaining fur-trapping areas open, McLoughlin directed Kelley, Wyeth, and the others to safety in the Willamette Valley near the modern capital of Salem. Former trappers who had married and settled down to farm also lived in the valley. Except for the huge white cone of Mount Hood in the distance, the region looked much like eastern farmland to the new arrivals. Word of the Willamette Valley soon spread east.

A Sad Prediction

Among the people who journeyed to Oregon with Hall Kelley, Nathaniel Wyeth, and missionaries Jason and Daniel Lee was scientist John Townsend. When he reached Oregon, Townsend understood why a growing number of Americans wanted to settle in Oregon. The land was incredibly fertile and rich. He wrote in his journal, "Wheat thrives here; I never saw better in any country, and . . . vegetables are in great profusion, and of the [highest] quality."

Of course, Native Americans far outnumbered white settlers in 1834. And, like most white men, Townsend thought of the original inhabitants as "savages." Of the Native Americans in Oregon, Townsend predicted "in a very few years the race will become extinct; and the time is probably not far distant when the trinkets of this people will be mementos of a nation passed forever from the face of the earth." ▪

In 1836, another group of missionaries and adventurers made its way to Oregon. For the first time, women came along. Marcus Whitman, his wife, Narcissa, and another couple settled in the upper Columbia River region and set up a mission in the land of the Nez Perce, the Cayuse, and other groups.

Marcus (left) and Narcissa Whitman

By the late 1830s, fewer than one hundred white settlers lived in Oregon. However, those people had grand ideas. At a meeting in 1838, the settlers wrote a petition to the U.S. Congress asking to be granted status as a U.S. territory—the first step toward becoming a state.

The missionary Jason Lee took the petition and rode east on horseback, stopping along the way to speak of the wonders of Oregon—the rich soil, the mild climate, and the wide-open lands of the Willamette Valley. Lee's timing could not have been better. By 1838, the United States had fallen into a deep economic depres-

The lush Willamette Valley was a lure to settlers.

John McLoughlin, or "the White-Headed Eagle"

At 6 feet 4 inches (193 cm) tall, he towered over most men of his time. His thick hair was white as snow. For more than two decades he controlled most of the vast Oregon country. Native Americans called him the White-Headed Eagle, but his given name was John McLoughlin.

McLoughlin was born in Quebec in 1784 and became a doctor at age nineteen. He journeyed west as a fur trader and doctor for the North West Company. In 1824, the North West Company was taken over by the larger Hudson's Bay Company, and McLoughlin was made director of a company outpost. Under his guidance, Fort Vancouver on the Columbia River became the largest trading center west of the Rocky Mountains.

McLoughlin's word was law to both whites and Native Americans, and he was widely respected for his intelligence and for his charity toward newcomers. McLoughlin always fed weary settlers and directed them to the safest land. One traveler wrote, "McLoughlin charged us nothing for supplies, gave us plenty of salmon and potatoes, and found us a house to stay in and even gave us firewood."

In 1845, McLoughlin retired to Oregon City and became a surveyor and builder. He built a house that is a national historic site today, and he became a U.S. citizen in 1849 while serving as the mayor of Oregon City. One hundred years after his death in 1857, Dr. John McLoughlin was named "Father of Oregon" by the state legislature. ■

sion. Banks had failed; land and crop prices had dropped. The promise of a new start in a land of fertile valleys and fair weather sounded good to Americans.

Lee delivered more than seventy-five speeches on his trip across the continent. Although Congress turned down the settlers' request to make Oregon a territory because there were too few people in its vast space, Lee distributed thousands of copies of the petition. In 1840, wagon trains gathered to make the journey to Oregon.

The Oregon Trail

What is known today as the Oregon Trail, one of the main routes west for pioneers, ran from Independence, Missouri, to Fort Vancouver, which is a distance of about 2,000 miles (3,200 km). The journey had to be completed in a five- or six-month period between spring and autumn before snow blocked the mountain passes.

A settler named Joel Walker is believed to have been the first person to make the complete trip with his family in 1840. However,

As many as 300,000 settlers moved west during the mid-1800s.

the well-known wagon trains began their westward movement, called the "great emigration," in 1843, when a group of more than 800 people with 120 wagons and 5,000 cattle made the trip in about five months.

Life on a wagon-train journey could be boring or exciting, pleasant or deadly. At dawn, livestock was rounded up and the oxen or mules were yoked to their wagons. After a breakfast of bacon and beans, the train guide, usually an old trapper or mountain man, along with scouts, who were sometimes Native Americans from the area, would set out on horseback to find the safest stream crossings and stake out the next night's campground.

When the wagon train stopped for a few hours at noon to allow the animals to rest, the settlers ate more bacon or some dried buffalo meat. On flat, dry land, a wagon train could make 20 miles (32 km) on a good day. In rough terrain or over mountains, the distance covered was much less. Cooking was done over fires of dried buffalo droppings because there were few trees on the plains.

Although many settlers on the journey had heard stories of Native American attacks, few actually occurred. For the most part, relations between settlers and Native Americans were peaceful. Some Indians acted as guides, and others were hired to help get wagons across swollen streams. Settlers often traded metal goods such as pots or fishhooks for fresh game or other foods.

Historians believe that more than 300,000 people made the trip on the Oregon Trail from the 1840s to the 1860s. As growing numbers of Americans made their way west, the trail became clearly marked. Even today, in an area not far from Laramie, Wyoming, wagon-wheel ruts left on the trail are 5 feet (1.5 m) deep.

What to Bring?

Preparing to travel the Oregon Trail took many months of planning. The idea was to travel light and bring easily preserved foods. Supplies (such as above) in each wagon had to weigh less than 2,000 pounds (908 kg) or the oxen would work themselves to death.

The basic foods were flour, crackers, bacon, sugar, coffee, tea, beans, rice, dried fruit, salt, pepper, and baking soda. Many families took along cows for fresh milk, and it wasn't unusual to see a small chicken coop hanging off a wagon to supply fresh eggs and meat. Men often hunted game to add to the bland diet.

Skillets, pots, and kettles were packed along with tin plates and eating implements. The settlers brought pottery crocks, canteens, and buckets as well as candles, matches, and soap. They carried tools to repair broken-down wagons; powder, lead, and shot for their guns; and basic tools such as shovels and axes.

Most people had two or three sets of sturdy wool clothing, so a sewing kit was important. Bedding and tents were the final necessities. For a family, these supplies usually came to about 1,800 pounds (817 kg). There was very little room for treasures such as books, furniture, or fancy clothing. Outfitting a basic wagon cost between $600 and $800. ■

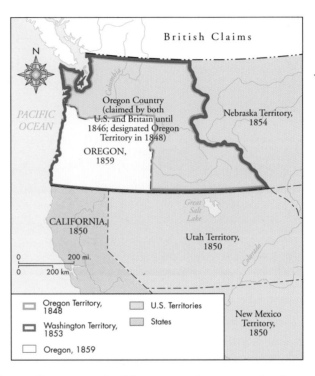

British Claims

N

PACIFIC
OCEAN

Oregon Country
(claimed by both
U.S. and Britain until
1846; designated Oregon
Territory in 1848)

OREGON,
1859

Nebraska Territory,
1854

CALIFORNIA,
1850

Great
Salt
Lake

Utah Territory,
1850

0   200 mi.

0   200 km

Oregon Territory,
1848

Washington Territory,
1853

Oregon, 1859

U.S. Territories

States

New Mexico
Territory,
1850

**Historical map
of Oregon**

But the trail was marked by more than ruts. In that same area near Laramie stands the grave of Joel Hembree, a six-year-old who died in 1843, crushed beneath the wheels of a wagon. It is the oldest marked grave on the trail. As the land became steeper across the Rockies, the road became littered with furniture, tools, and even food tossed out to make the wagons lighter.

Historians believe that about 10 percent of those who set out on the Oregon Trail died on the way—between 20,000 and 30,000 people. Some, like Joel Hembree, were crushed beneath the wheels of a heavy wagon, many died in other accidents or drowned in swift-flowing rivers. But the biggest killer by far was disease. Sanitation was poor and medical knowledge was limited.

Cholera, an infectious intestinal disease caused by drinking

The Whitman Massacre

Like most missionaries who traveled west to Oregon, Marcus Whitman and his wife, Narcissa, hoped to teach the Native Americans about Christianity. They set up their mission in eastern Oregon country among the Cayuse people. Marcus Whitman was a doctor and a pioneer as well as a preacher.

He and Narcissa (who, along with Eliza Spalding, was one of the first white women to travel west of the Rockies) lived on Cayuse land from 1837 until 1847. During the migration west in the early 1840s, wagon trains stopped at the mission before making the final push across Oregon. In 1843, the Whitmans adopted seven orphaned children whose parents had died on the Oregon Trail. By 1847, more than seventy people lived at the Whitman mission (shown above).

Measles, a disease unknown to the Cayuse, struck the village in 1847. Despite the settlers' efforts to save lives, hundreds of Cayuse died.

Unfortunately, it was a Cayuse custom to kill medicine men who failed. On a June morning in 1847, while standing at his door, Marcus Whitman was killed by a tomahawk blow to the back of the head. Shots rang out and the residents of the mission fled into the main house while Cayuse warriors surrounded it.

A Cayuse chief stepped forward and told Narcissa Whitman that the warriors planned to burn down the mission. If the people inside came out, he said, they would be escorted safely off Cayuse land. It was a trick. As soon as the settlers were outside, the Cayuse shot them. Narcissa Whitman and sixteen other people died, including two of the orphaned children. The mission was destroyed. More than fifty settlers were kidnapped and later freed for ransom.

The Whitman Massacre led to the first war between Oregon settlers and Native Americans. Five Cayuse were taken back to Oregon City and tried for murder. They were executed in 1850. News of the Whitman Massacre traveled east and caused an increase in the tension between the settlers moving west and the Native Americans who already lived there. ■

unclean water, claimed many lives. At that time, no one knew that simply boiling water before drinking it kills bacteria. And many settlers, exhausted by the long trip, died of influenza, food poisoning, or a tick-carried disease known as "mountain fever."

Until 1848, the Oregon country was said to begin when the Rockies were crossed. But for many, the real sense of reaching Oregon came once they had crossed the dangerous Snake River in modern-day eastern Oregon. From that point, most settlers traveled north to the Columbia River, passing the mission of Marcus Whitman and stopping at the Dalles, a fort on the river's

President James Knox Polk was in office in 1848 when the Oregon Territory was created.

rapids operated by John McLoughlin. Newcomers often had their first taste of Pacific salmon there.

But the hazards of the journey were far from over. From the Dalles, settlers rolled their wagons onto flatboats belonging to the Hudson's Bay Company to float downriver to Fort Vancouver. Rapids and waterfalls claimed many lives. During one of the first wagon-train voyages, two boys of the Applegate family drowned when their flatboat overturned. The grief-stricken family later discovered a southern route across Oregon country known as the Applegate Trail.

By 1846, so many Americans had settled in Oregon that the British decided to give up their claim to the region below the 49th parallel, which is the northern border of Washington state today. In 1848, President James Polk signed a bill creating Oregon Territory, which included the present states of Oregon, Washington, and Idaho as well as western regions of Montana and Wyoming. By 1849, Oregon established a territorial government in Oregon City along the Willamette River.

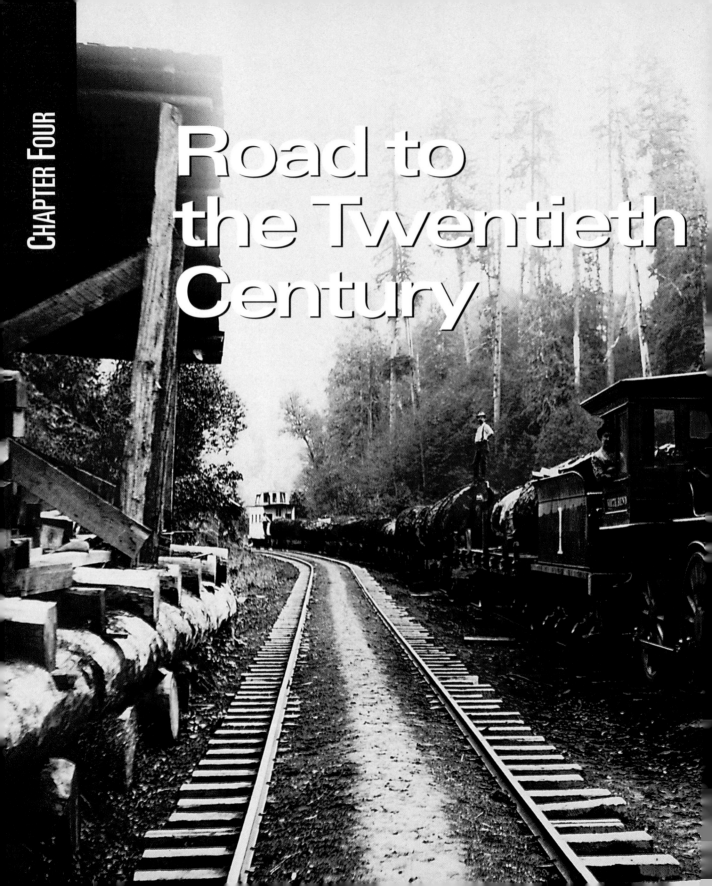

CHAPTER FOUR

Road to the Twentieth Century

By 1848, the year Oregon became a territory, about 13,000 settlers lived in Oregon, mainly in the Willamette Valley. The first governor of the territory, Joseph Lane, established the capital at Oregon City. Over the next several years, two events would bring thousands more settlers to live in Oregon.

Gold was discovered at Sutter's Mill in northern California early in 1848. News of the discovery spread slowly to the East Coast, but once it did, the numbers of newcomers exploded. Although some miners, nicknamed 49ers after 1849, the year they arrived, did strike paydirt in California, most did not. Many of those who made their fortunes in California remained in the West because the U.S. Congress passed the Oregon Donation Land Law in 1850. Under that law, any citizen who had farmed in Oregon for four years would receive 320 acres (129 hectares) of land. A married man would be given an additional 320 acres. And those who came after 1850 were immediately eligible for up to 320 acres of land.

In much of the expanding United States, the land that Congress "gave away" had been the homeland of Native Americans for centuries. Waves of settlers came to Oregon, bringing with them a way of life—farming—that was different from the hunting, fishing, and gathering traditions of Native Americans. Whites also brought

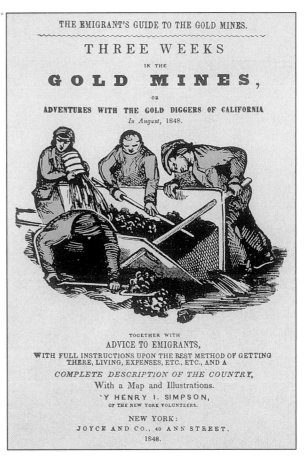

THE EMIGRANT'S GUIDE TO THE GOLD MINES.

THREE WEEKS IN THE GOLD MINES, OR ADVENTURES WITH THE GOLD DIGGERS OF CALIFORNIA In August, 1848.

TOGETHER WITH ADVICE TO EMIGRANTS, WITH FULL INSTRUCTIONS UPON THE BEST METHOD OF GETTING THERE, LIVING, EXPENSES, ETC., ETC., AND A COMPLETE DESCRIPTION OF THE COUNTRY, With a Map and Illustrations. BY HENRY I. SIMPSON, OF THE NEW YORK VOLUNTEERS.

NEW YORK: JOYCE AND CO., 40 ANN STREET, 1848.

The promise of wealth in the new gold fields was particularly appealing to poor immigrants from the East.

Opposite: An Oregon log train in 1880

Chief Joseph

something else with them—disease. Measles, smallpox, and influenza killed huge numbers of Native Americans in Oregon. The population of coastal tribes in Oregon fell 50 percent between 1850 and 1900.

By the mid-1850s, most Indians of the Willamette Valley had been sent to reservations. Being forced onto barren land—sometimes with tribes who were long-time enemies—spelled disaster for the Native Americans of Oregon. Over the next twenty years, wars broke out between settlers and Native American tribes throughout Oregon.

The most terrible conflict occurred in 1877 when settlers tried to move the Nez Perce people off their lands in eastern Oregon and onto a reservation. Angry warriors rebelled and killed eighteen settlers. Led by Chief Joseph, a band of about 450 men, women, and children then retreated through what are now Idaho and Montana.

For more than 1,000 miles (1,609 km), the U.S. Cavalry chased the Nez Perce. Chief Joseph and his warriors defeated the troops several times until the Indians were trapped 30 miles (48 km) south of the Canadian border. Finally, with winter fast approaching, Chief Joseph surrendered with these words, "I am tired of fighting. . . . The little children are freezing to death. . . . From where the sun now stands I will fight no more forever." He died in 1904 on a Nez Perce reservation, it is said, of a broken heart.

Gold Fever Strikes Oregon

Because news of the January 1848 gold strike in California did not reach the East Coast until late that year, Oregon settlers had a head start. In July 1848, a captain sailing north from San Francisco to Fort Vancouver brought word of the gold strike. Within months, two-thirds of all the men in Oregon had headed south.

Farming and other responsibilities were forgotten. The Oregon legislature was unable to meet because more than half of its members had left for California. The state's only newspaper, the *Oregon Spectator*, did not publish an edition from September 7 until October 12, 1848. The paper reappeared with an apology, "The Spectator, after a temporary sickness, greets its patrons and hopes to serve them faithfully. The 'gold fever,' [sweeping] . . . through Oregon . . . took away our printers."

A few Oregonians struck it rich, but most went back to the Willamette Valley before the first 49ers arrived. Once they returned, the money began to come in. The fertile farmlands and thick forests of the Willamette produced food and lumber for people in California who were too busy mining to farm or build.

Roads between Oregon and California improved, and gold poured into the territory at the rate of about $2 million a year. Wheat ground into flour for 65¢ a bushel (.0352 cu m) in Oregon sold for $9 a bushel in California. Apples sold for $1.50 *each* in California—about $15 in today's money. By the early 1850s, Oregon apple growers were sending 20,000 bushels (720 cu m) of apples a year to California. So much gold made its way into Oregon that it was said you could run a toothpick between the floorboards of any saloon and pick up $50 worth of gold dust. ◼

Slavery and the Civil War

During the first half of the nineteenth century, the question of slavery tore at the fabric of the United States. As territories were settled by newcomers from the North and South, the decision to remain a slave or free state was fiercely—and sometimes violently—debated.

In Oregon, territorial lawmakers had passed laws banning all African-Americans, slave or free, in the late 1840s. As a result of the so-called Exclusion Law, very few blacks were living in Oregon when the territory became a nonslave state in 1859.

Because of laws that banned African-Americans, few blacks were able to take advantage of Oregon Territory's vast, fertile lands.

Exclusion Law or not, the tensions leading up to the Civil War did not bypass Oregon. A number of settlers, including many prospectors who had found gold in the Rogue River area, wanted to establish a separate proslavery state in southern Oregon and northern California. The movement was voted down, but the attitude of many whites in Oregon drove most African-Americans across the U.S. border to British Columbia in Canada.

Economic Growth

The bloody battles of the Civil War did not actually touch Oregon, but the war had a significant impact on Oregon's economy. With

large herds of sheep grazing on farms in the Willamette Valley, Oregon had a large supply of wool, and Union troops needed blankets and other woolen goods. The city of Salem, which became the state capital in 1859, was the main textile-producing city in Oregon.

Horses and a reaper after a day of harvesting wheat, circa 1880

In addition to woolen goods, Oregon became a major exporter of agricultural products such as wheat. By 1880, a fleet of cargo ships was carrying millions of bushels of grain to England, Australia, and China.

The main problem facing farmers and merchants in Oregon was delivering goods to eastern states. Even though the transcontinental railroad had been completed in 1869, no railroads connected the

A Timeline of African-American History in Oregon

1788 Marcus Lopez, cabin boy of Captain Robert Gray, becomes the first person of African descent known to have set foot in Oregon.

1805 York, William Clark's slave, travels west with the Lewis and Clark expedition.

1844 Slavery is declared illegal in the Oregon country. The brutal Lash Law, requiring that blacks—slave or free—be whipped twice a year "until he or she quit the territory" is passed in June. The law is changed that December to a punishment of forced labor.

1851 Jacob Vanderpool, owner of a boardinghouse in Salem, becomes the only known person of color to be kicked out of Oregon Territory because of his skin color.

1859 Oregon becomes the first state admitted to the Union with an exclusion law banning African-Americans on its books.

1862 Oregon adopts a law requiring all blacks, Asians, and people of mixed race to pay a yearly tax of five dollars. Those who cannot pay are sentenced to forced labor on state roads.

1868 The Fourteenth Amendment granting citizenship to African-Americans passes in Oregon.

1870 The Fifteenth Amendment, granting African-American men the right to vote is added to the U.S. Constitution, although it fails to pass in Oregon. The amendment becomes law, but it is not approved in Oregon until 1959—the state's centennial.

1914 The Portland chapter of the National Association for the Advancement of Colored People (NAACP), the oldest chapter west of the Mississippi River, is founded.

1926 Oregon repeals its exclusion law.

"Greasing the Skids"

The enormous logs from the Oregon forests were too heavy to be dragged along flat ground. Shorter, smaller logs were laid side to side in a roadway to make it easier for oxen or horses to pull huge the logs to a river or railway. The logs that made up the roadway were called "skids."

Even with skids, pulling the logs was difficult, so young boys were hired to run ahead of the team and cover the skids with lard to help the logs slide. This job was known as "greasing the skids," and that expression came to mean "making something easier" in everyday English.

Willamette Valley with states on the eastern side of the Rocky Mountains. The chief method of transport was by water, up the Willamette River to the town of Portland. From there, ships carried goods down the Columbia River and then followed the coast south to San Francisco, where the railroad sent shipments across the country.

Railways connecting Oregon with eastern states were finally completed in the 1880s, and goods produced in the state could then be transported by rail to large cities east of the Rockies. It was much easier to get to Oregon once the railroads were complete—the Oregon Trail became a distant memory as waves of immigrants arrived by rail.

These immigrants found that much of the land in the Willamette Valley had been taken by early settlers. As a result, many newcomers in the late 1800s either settled in cities such as Portland or moved east of the Cascade Range to ranch or farm.

Logging became a major industry in Oregon during the late 1800s. The thick forests of Douglas fir—many standing 200 feet

Fir trees were the basis of Oregon's logging business.

(61 m) tall—on the Coast Range and the Cascade Range became a valuable resource for the state and for the country as a whole. Steam-powered engines called "donkeys" were used to haul trees off steep slopes. Oxen or horses then dragged logs to the nearest river or railroad. Some trees were so large that it took a team of twenty oxen to pull one log. For those in the lumber and logging industry, the supply of trees seemed endless.

Entering the Twentieth Century

Oregon's economy, with its fertile land and abundant natural resources, was healthy as it approached its fiftieth anniversary as a state. On the eastern plateau, cattle ranches and wheat farms prospered. In the west, the Cascades provided ponderosa pine and Douglas fir for logging. The fertile Willamette Valley supplied

food for many regions. And the fishing industry—especially the salmon catch—kept the coastal economy healthy.

As Oregon's seventy-fifth anniversary approached, however, dark clouds hung over the whole country. In 1929, the U.S. economy began to fall apart, and the 1930s came to be known as the decade of the Great Depression. Stocks fell, banks failed, and drought in the Midwest spelled disaster for millions of farmers.

The depression years caused great changes in Oregon's economy. In 1933, the newly elected president, Franklin D. Roosevelt, developed a plan for economic recovery called the New Deal. It included many conservation projects that put jobless people to

As the nineteenth century ended, Oregon thrived off its land and industry.

"Stumptown"

Until the 1860s, the city of Portland was a small town located 100 miles (160 km) up the Columbia River where it joins the Willamette River. In early 1860, gold was discovered in several areas of eastern Oregon, Idaho, and Montana. Although the amount of gold was not as great as that discovered in California, the rush for riches brought thousands of miners to the region. In order to reach the gold fields, miners had to travel east up the Columbia River.

A group of business leaders met this need by forming the Oregon Steam Navigation Company in Portland, making it the main west to east connection for travelers. Portland grew so rapidly that, as trees were cut down to make streets, there was no time to remove the stumps. When rains made the streets muddy, Portlanders made their way by jumping from stump to stump. The stumps were even painted white to make them easier to see. As a result, one of the city's early nicknames was "Stumptown." ■

work. In Oregon, agencies such as the Works Progress Administration (WPA) and the Civilian Conservation Corps (CCC) replanted logged-out forests, irrigated desert areas, and constructed flood-control gates on rivers. Many of Oregon's highways and recreational areas were developed during the 1930s by WPA and CCC workers.

The most important New Deal project for Oregon took more than six years to build. The Bonneville Dam, completed in 1937, was built across the Columbia River about 40 miles (64 km) east of Portland. The powerful current of the Columbia River was now tamed and provided electricity to people throughout the Northwest as well as to industries in Portland.

World War II

The electric power generated by the Bonneville Dam brought many changes to Oregon when the United States entered World War II in 1941. With such a convenient source of electricity, Portland became one of the largest shipbuilding cities in the United States. The aluminum industry began to thrive in the area as well.

As did other states on the West Coast of the United States, Oregon participated in one of the most unfortunate aspects of World War II—the relocation of Japanese Americans. The threat of Japan invading America's western coast caused President Roosevelt and other American leaders to assume that Japanese Ameri-

The energy from Bonneville Dam assisted Portland in becoming the city it is today.

cans were a security risk. In 1942, President Roosevelt ordered all people of Japanese ancestry living west of the Cascade Range to move east. These people, many of whom had lived in America for years, were forced into relocation centers in California, Idaho, Wyoming, and eastern Oregon.

During the war, a Japanese submarine fired at Fort Stevens, a military base at the mouth of the Columbia River. And in 1945 a Japanese bomb attached to a balloon floated into an Oregon coastal area and killed a family on a picnic. These two incidents were the only attacks on the American mainland by enemy forces during World War II.

When the war ended, many Japanese Americans returned to their homes to find all of their belongings gone, their life savings lost, and their land overgrown. They often faced racial prejudice in the years immediately after the war. In 1988, the U.S. Congress awarded $20,000 to each Japanese American who had been sent to a relocation center during World War II.

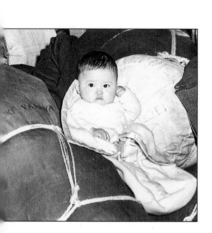

This nine-month-old Japanese-American baby was moved to an assembly center in Portland in 1942.

A Love of the Land

The last half of the twentieth century has brought Oregon to the front of the effort to preserve the environment. No matter what their political views, most Oregonians are united in their love for the great natural beauty and resources of their state. During the 1960s, citizens began to take steps to preserve and protect that beauty.

In 1967, laws were passed that controlled the amount of pollution that industries could dump into the Willamette River. In the same year, Oregon became the first state to ban aluminum cans with pull-off openers. In 1971, one of the nation's first "bottle

bills"—banning no-deposit, nonrecyclable beverage bottles—was made into law. And in 1975, Oregon became the first state to ban aerosol cans containing fluorocarbons, chemicals believed to destroy the earth's ozone layer.

Now, as Oregon marks nearly a century and a half of statehood, its people look proudly back at the past of trappers and traders and Oregon Trail pioneers. They look to the future with the same spirit of daring and determination.

The citizens of Oregon recognize the value of preserving the land around them.

CHAPTER FIVE

A State Shaped by Mountains

The Oregon coast
between Newport
and Florence

With its rugged coastlines and green valleys, its snowy peaks, vast plateaus, and sun-baked deserts, Oregon has one of America's most diverse and striking landscapes. The state's picturesque western border is formed by the Pacific Ocean. Its northern border with Washington state is marked mainly by the Columbia River. To the south are the mountains of California and the deserts of Nevada. To the east, the Snake River forms much of Oregon's eastern border with Idaho.

Oregon is a state divided by mountains. On the western edge of the state are the Coast Range, including the Klamath Mountains. Inland, the spectacular Cascade Range runs the entire length of Oregon. These mountain ranges, which absorb much of the moisture and precipitation moving off the ocean, create two distinct climates. West of the Cascades, Oregon's climate is moist and mild; east of the Cascades, on the high plateau and in the desert regions, the climate is dry and often displays extreme temperature ranges. Within its borders, the state has a variety of land regions, many

Opposite: Autumn
in Mount Hood
National Forest

A State Shaped by Mountains **57**

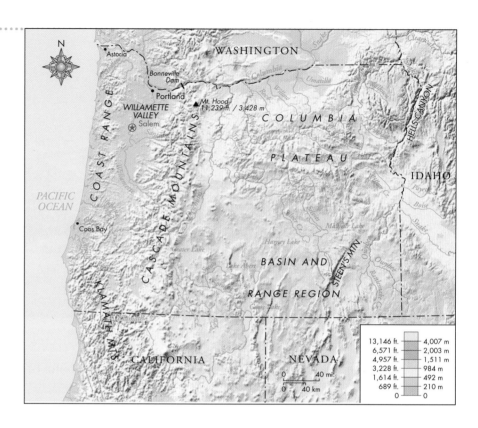

Oregon's topography

rivers, and some of the most awe-inspiring scenery in the United States.

The most widely recognized landmark in Oregon is majestic Mount Hood, a peak in the Cascade Range that towers 11,239 feet (3,428 m) over the skyline of Portland, the state's largest city. Like many peaks in the Cascade Range, Mount Hood is an extinct volcano. Among the other notable mountains in the Cascades are the Three Sisters, volcanic cones that have been extinct for at least 12,000 years.

The Coastal Region

Oregon's coast has few natural harbors or bays. Its 367-mile (591-km) shoreline is made up of long stretches of beach inter-

Haystock Rock at Cape Kiwanda State Park

rupted by cliffs overlooking the waters of the Pacific. All along the coast, spires of rock called sea stacks jut from the water like giant teeth. The entire region is walled off by the Coast Range. These ridges of volcanic rock form narrow, steep gorges that run north to south along the ocean, keeping the region cool and moist almost year-round. Fog and mist bring an air of mystery to this lightly populated area.

Oregon's Geographical Features

Total area; rank	97,131 sq. mi. (251,569 sq km); 10th
Land; rank	96,002 sq. mi. (248,645 sq km); 10th
Water; rank	1,129 sq. mi. (2,927 sq km); 26th
Inland water; **rank**	1,049 sq. mi. (2,717 sq km); 19th
Coastal water; **rank**	80 sq. mi. (207 sq km); 19th
Geographic center	Crook, 25 miles (40 km) southeast of Prineville
Highest point	Mount Hood, 11,239 feet (3,428 km) above sea level
Lowest point	Sea level along the coastline
Largest city	Portland
Population; rank	2,853,733 (1990 census); 29th
Record high temperature	119°F (48°C) at Prineville on July 29, 1898, and at Pendleton on August 10, 1898
Record low temperature	−54°F (−48°C) at Ukiah on February 9, 1933, and at Seneca on February 10, 1933
Average July temperature	66°F (19°C)
Average January temperature	32°F (0°C)
Annual precipitation	28 inches (71 cm)

Coos Bay and Astoria are the only two towns on the coast with populations greater than 10,000. Coos Bay is the leading ocean harbor for freighters on the Oregon coast, many of which carry softwood from the forests of Douglas fir that cover the western mountainsides. It's easy to see why most people here earn their living in the logging or fishing industries. Many visitors enjoy vacationing on the coast too, and tourism is important to the area's economy. More than seventy state parks and a large area of U.S. government–owned land preserve the wild beauty of the coast for nature lovers.

Oregonians are proud of their coast and have passed laws to preserve its natural beauty. Legislation and the windy climate of the

Oregon's Lighthouses

For centuries, explorers sailing along the rugged Oregon coast were turned away from land by fog and foul weather. In 1892, the first lighthouse was built at the point where the Umpqua River meets the Pacific.

Other lighthouses built before the turn of the century include the Hecata Head Light (right), named after the Spanish explorer who first sighted the Columbia River and claimed it for Spain in 1775. The light, high on jagged rocks, was built by floating lumber along the coast on rafts to the base of the cliffs, then hauling it up the rock face.

Another well-known lighthouse, built in 1870 at Tillamook Rock, sits 1.5 miles (2.4 km) offshore on a monstrous sea stack. The light was known as "Terrible Tilly" because the first surveyor to inspect the rock drowned when he was swept away by a huge wave. ■

area have created wide-open spaces such as the federally protected Oregon dunes. These rolling hills of sand were formed when sediment washed down from the surrounding mountains. Unlike harder volcanic rock, sediment is crushed to sand by powerful ocean waves, then washed back on shore. Strong northwest winds carry the sand as far as 2 miles (3.2 km) inland. This 41-mile (66-km) stretch north of Coos Bay attracts hikers and other fans of the outdoors who don't mind the stiff wind blowing off the ocean.

The Willamette Valley

Inland of the Coast Range lies the beautiful Willamette Valley. The Willamette River, 309 miles (497 km) long, winds its way north through the valley to the Columbia River, adding the finishing touch to one of the most scenic areas in the United States. With its mild climate, good soil, and natural beauty, the valley became a

The Tillamook Burn

People around the northern coastal town of Tillamook still talk about the Tillamook Burn of 1933, one of the most destructive forest fires in history. During that fire, a 15-foot (4.6-m) wall of flame leaped to ignite trees that were 150 feet (46 m) tall. Ships that were 500 miles (805 km) out at sea were coated with ash from the fire. The fire destroyed enough lumber to build a million five-bedroom houses—more than 240,000 acres (97,200 ha).

Today, the Tillamook Burn is green once again. Nature, along with one of the largest forest-rehabilitation projects ever undertaken, has covered the scars.

favored location for early settlers. Today, 70 percent of Oregonians live in this lovely valley, nestled among the coastal mountains, the Klamath Mountains in the southeast, and the Cascades in the east.

The Willamette Valley is about 115 miles (185 km) long and up to 30 miles (48 km) wide. Within this region, more than eighty different crops are grown and harvested—from onions and beans to grapes and strawberries. The climate, with almost 48 inches (122 cm) of rain a year, is ideal for growing fruit and nut trees. The valley is the nation's leading supplier of hazelnuts, as well as blackberries, peppermint, and grass seed.

The Willamette River is fed by many smaller rivers and streams that create natural irrigation fields for the land. In addition, the extinct volcanoes of the nearby Cascade Range supply deep layers of ash, a natural fertilizer, from past eruptions.

Tulips are among the many plants that thrive in the fertile Willamette Valley.

The Columbia Plateau

Northeast of the Willamette Valley, past the western slopes of the Cascade Range, is the Columbia Plateau. This region of Oregon was formed by huge rivers of volcanic lava that flowed from the fissures and vents that once covered the area. This enormous region covers nearly one-fourth of the state and is less mountainous than the rest. However, the craggy Blue Mountains contain many beautiful snowcapped peaks and lakes formed by melting glaciers.

Because the good farmland of the Columbia Plateau is less expensive than land in the Willamette Valley, farms are larger. Here, wheat is grown in both the winter and spring. Much of it is shipped down the Columbia River to Portland and from there to countries in Asia.

There are also cattle and sheep ranches on the plateau. Much of the grasslands and forests are owned by the federal government, which permits local ranchers to graze livestock there.

Many smaller rivers in the plateau flow north to the Columbia River. As in the Willamette Valley, these rivers irrigate fields of sugar beets and potatoes.

Part of the state's northeastern border with Idaho is formed by the Snake River. One of the most awesome sights on the river is Hell's Canyon. Over millions of years, the Snake River has knifed

Sheep graze on grasslands throughout Oregon.

through the volcanic rock, forming the deepest gorge in North America. At certain locations, Hell's Canyon is more than 7,000 feet (2,135 m) deep.

The Snake River as it runs through Hell's Canyon

The Great Basin

East of the Cascades, southeast Oregon is one of the hottest, coldest, and driest areas of the entire northwestern United States. Geologists call this "high desert," but the settlers called it the Great Basin—the name it is known by today. The Great Basin makes up

Bison in Hell's Canyon

Visitors to Hell's Canyon in northeastern Oregon can see the animal that has grazed on these grasslands at the foot of the Blue Mountains for as long as anyone can say. A herd of American bison, or buffalo—the largest mammals in North America—are raised at Hell's Canyon Bison Ranch.

The bison, which feed on grass and grass hay, are up to 10 feet (3 m) long and 6 feet (1.8 m) tall and weigh more than 1,000 pounds (454 kg). Bison love cold weather, and their fur grows thick and shaggy during the colder months.

The bison are raised to be eaten. With half the calories of beef, bison meat is becoming increasingly popular across the United States. ■

about one-fourth of Oregon, but only about 1 percent of the population lives there.

In many parts of the Great Basin, less than 10 inches (25 cm) of rain falls per year. Names such as Malheur (French for "bad luck"), Poverty Flat, Starvation Spring, Deadman's Bedground, and Skull Creek give us an idea of the hardships faced by the first settlers. Not only is the basin dry, but temperatures range from over 100°F (38°C) in summer to –30°F (–34°C) in winter.

A notable landmark in this mostly flat area is Steen's Mountain, which rises like a giant's backbone more than 9,600 feet (2,928 m) over the Alvord Desert region of the basin. This mountain—called a massif by geologists—is more than 30 miles (48 km) long. The road that runs around it is longer than the border between Connecticut and Rhode Island.

In the center of the basin lies the Malheur National Wildlife Refuge. Oddly enough, Malheur Lake is Oregon's largest natural

body of water, though its size varies because of evaporation and the amount of yearly rainfall. Sometimes it covers more than 180,000 acres (72,900 ha) of shallow marshland and water, and other times it is just a huge dry mud hole.

The wildlife refuge is one of the main flyway stopovers for birds migrating south from Canada. Large numbers of raptors such as bald eagles and peregrine falcons can be seen here. And each autumn more than 3,000 sandhill cranes, with wingspans up

Steen's Mountain is a beautiful landmark in the Great Basin.

to 7.5 feet (2.3 m), stop at the refuge to feed on grains before continuing on to California.

The Columbia River

The Columbia River, which forms more than two-thirds of the boundary between Oregon and Washington, has been a lifeline for people of the Northwest for centuries. In the years before Europeans arrived, Native Americans stood on platforms over the roar-

Sunrise on the Columbia River

ing river, using long-handled nets to harvest salmon swimming upstream.

In the 1840s, wagon trains that reached the Columbia had to float downstream on rafts to Fort Vancouver before reaching the Willamette Valley. Because the river slopes toward the Pacific, its powerful currents create many deadly stretches of white water and rapids. Journals of traveling west on the Oregon Trail often tell of tragedies on this final leg of the trip.

In 1937, the Bonneville Dam was built on the Columbia. In the decades since, more than fifty dams and irrigation projects have diverted the enormous power of its flowing water to bring electricity (which is important for irrigation) to the Northwest. Today, hydroelectric plants on the Columbia River provide electricity for people in seven states. More than 50 million tons of cargo move down the river every year. And though the many waterfalls and rapids have been tamed, salmon still return upriver in their timeless pattern.

Plants and Animals

The forests of Oregon are a major part of the state's identity. Forests cover more than 40 percent of the land, and Oregon has been the largest producer of lumber in the United States since 1938. Because of the number of trees cut, preservation is still a concern.

The wildflowers of Oregon welcome drivers, bikers, and hikers. Bright blue delphiniums, the rainbow colors of the Indian paintbrush, and the rich hues of the glacier lily are among the many wildflowers that delight visitors.

Trees of Oregon

The Douglas fir is the state tree, and these towering evergreens carpet the western slopes of Oregon's mountains. The conifers of the Pacific Coast are among the oldest trees in North America.

Other hardwood and softwood trees have reached tremendous sizes in the state's moist climate and rich soil. Oregon is home to several of the largest trees in the United States, measured by size. The champs are:

Bigleaf Maple: 34 feet 11 inches wide (10.6 m); 101 feet (30.8 m) tall

Black Walnut: 23 feet 2 inches (7.1 m) wide; 130 feet (39.7 m) tall

California White Fir: 19 feet 3 inches (5.9 m) wide; 175 feet (53.4 m) tall

Coastal Douglas Fir (left): 36 feet 6 inches (11.1 m) wide; 329 feet (100.3 m) tall

Ponderosa Pine: 28 feet 6 inches (8.7 m) wide; 178 feet (54.3 m) tall

Port Orford Cedar: 37 feet 7 inches (11.5 m) wide; 219 feet (66.8 m) tall

Sitka Spruce: 56 feet 1 inches (17.1 m) wide; 206 feet (62.8 m) tall

The Willamette Valley's moist, mild climate creates the perfect environment for roses. In fact, the nickname of Portland, the state's largest city, is the Rose City. Roses were brought there by the first settlers and now bloom year-round.

Because the state is so large, and its climates so diverse, a wide variety of wildlife live in Oregon. It is home to North America's largest rodent, the beaver, as well as smaller animals such as rabbits, skunks, raccoons, chipmunks, and squirrels.

Larger wild animals in Oregon include deer, elk, and antelope. Bears and cougars—also called mountain lions—are numerous too. Game birds that provided food for the Native Americans and first settlers include pheasant and bobwhite quail.

Over the past few decades, two endangered species of wildlife, the spotted owl and the salmon, have become symbols of the controversy between environmentalists and business interests. The

Oregon's parks and forests

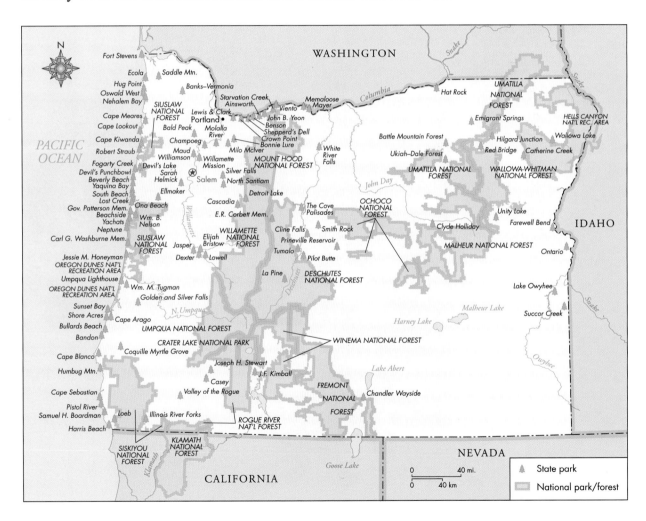

The spotted owl has been at the center of environmental controversy.

spotted owl needs old-growth forests to survive, so logging corporations are forbidden to cut certain areas of timber. Salmon need unobstructed waterfalls and rapids to survive, but dams and power facilities on the Columbia and other rivers have destroyed salmon runs. Efforts are underway to reach an agreement between business interests and environmentalists over these problems.

Climate

Because Oregon is divided by mountains, the state has two completely different climates. West of the Cascade Range, the weather

Snowfall on a Christmas tree farm in Marion County

The Great Flood of 1996

In spite of Oregon's size and varied climates, the flood of 1996 affected the entire state. It was the worst flood in a hundred years. Most of Oregon's waterways overflowed and flooded all thirty-six counties with a huge surge of water.

The February flood washed out rural roads, stranding dozens of towns and causing hardships for hundreds of thousands of people. Eight deaths and more than fifty injuries resulted from the combination of heavy snowstorms followed by warming temperatures and torrential rain.

The floods turned low-lying coastal areas such as Tillamook into lakes. Dairy farmers lost hundreds of cattle. The Willamette River came within inches of overflowing into downtown Portland. Eighteen counties in Oregon were declared disaster areas and National Guard troops were called in to assist in evacuation and rescue.

What caused this devastating flood? Besides the snow and heavy rain, logging and road building may have contributed to the damage. Environmental experts believe that rivers and streams may increase flow more than 50 percent when the surrounding forest has been logged. ■

is mild and moist, while east of the Cascades, the high desert plateau varies from blistering heat to paralyzing cold. Oregon's record high and low temperatures have been set in this area.

Precipitation is highest on the coast, especially on the western slopes of the Coast Range. Rain and snowfall in that area exceeds 150 inches (381 cm) per year.

Eastern Oregon has an average precipitation of 10 to 20 inches (25 to 50 cm) per year. In the more arid desert regions of the Great Basin, less than 10 inches (25 cm) falls in an average year.

CHAPTER SIX

Here, There, Everywhere around Oregon

Seven out of ten Oregonians live in the Willamette Valley, nestled between the Coast Range and the Cascade Range. Most of these residents live in the greater metropolitan area surrounding Portland.

Because of its location near the junction of the Willamette and Columbia Rivers, Portland has become one of the major shipping ports in the Northwest. Cargo ships filled with wheat, lumber, and paper products line the docks. The number of Portland residents is nearing half a million, and the growth of surrounding towns in the greater metropolitan region, such as Beaverton and Hillsboro, have become among the fastest-growing regions in the United States.

It isn't just jobs or money that makes Portland one of America's most popular cities. Although it rains in Portland about 150 days a year, the city's mild climate and long growing season have created one of America's most beautiful big-city landscapes.

Portland's nickname is the Rose City. The police cars have a rose emblem on their doors. Its colorful flowers, gardens, and parks make the city a place of exceptional beauty. The Interna-

Full moon over downtown Portland, a major inland shipping port

Opposite: International Rose Test Gardens at Washington Park in Portland

Best for Bicyclists

For a number of years, Portland has been rated the top American city for bicyclists by *Bicycling* magazine. The city's residents and elected officials take bicycling seriously, says the magazine. Here's what they mean:

"Bike Central" in the heart of the city offers bike racks, showers, and lockers for a fee to anyone who wants to commute to work by bike. Free bicycle parking is offered at major city events and Portland has nearly 200 miles (322 km) of bike paths. ∎

tional Rose Test Gardens display more than 8,000 plants of 550 varieties of roses that bloom nearly year-round. Portland claims to have more garden clubs than any other city in America.

With its mild climate and natural beauty, Portland consistently makes the lists of the most livable cities in the United States. From its year-round flowers, to a Japanese garden near the downtown business district, to the miles of hiking and bike paths crisscrossing the city, Portland is an inviting destination for everyone.

But as any Oregonian will admit, there is much more to Oregon than Portland. Each city and town, no matter where it is located, has its own history and traditions. Museums displaying both Native American artifacts and pioneer relics can be found in almost every locale. Because many of the first settlers came from the East, much of the layout and architecture of Oregon's cities seems familiar to visitors from other parts of the United States.

The I-5 Corridor

Most of Oregon's population lives in the Willamette Valley, along Interstate 5, so the state's largest cities are located there. The second-largest city in Oregon—Eugene—is 75 miles (121 km) south of Portland on the Willamette River along what is called the I-5 corridor. Eugene has more than 112,000 residents, and the city adjoining it—Springfield—has a population of more than 40,000. The state capital, Salem, located between Portland and Eugene, has a population of about 107,000. Much of the history of the area is centered on the Willamette River and the Oregon Trail pioneers who arrived there in the 1840s.

Eugene is the second-largest city in Oregon.

Today, the Willamette Valley is a favorite spot for tourists and newcomers. The name of one river that meanders across the valley and flows into the Willamette says a lot about the feelings of the region's residents. The Tualatin River got its name from a Native American word meaning "slow and easy-flowing." That name also describes the way of life of the people who live in the valley.

Farmland in the Willamette Valley

In many ways, the open, flat farmland remains as picturesque today as it was in the 1800s. Residents of the cities along the Willamette value the natural beauty of their surroundings.

Like Portland, many of Oregon's largest cities have strong commitments to providing highly liveable communities to their citizens. Eugene, home of the University of Oregon, is dedicated to physical fitness, crossed by jogging paths and bike lanes.

Corvallis, with a population of more than 44,000, is the home of Oregon State University and another example of the ways in which Oregonians combine urban growth with respect for the beauty of the valley. The cities of the Willamette Valley remain favorite places to live and to visit because people there work to preserve the natural beauty of their environment.

Benton County Court-house in Corvallis

Coastal Oregon

The coast was settled last by white pioneers. It is an area of thick mists, steep canyons, and huge forests, and only two of its cities—Coos Bay and Astoria—have more than 10,000 people. However, the region that stretches 367 miles (591 km) from Brookings in the south to Astoria at the mouth of the Columbia River draws millions of visitors every year.

First City on the Willamette

Before settlers arrived in the 1840s, Native American groups often gathered at a location known as Hyas Tee Tumwater, where the Clackamas River joins the Willamette River. The falls—the Tumwater—was the location of Oregon City (right)—the largest city between California and Alaska at that time.

In the 1840s, the city at Willamette Falls was the final destination of Oregon Trail travelers. It became the home of Dr. John McLoughlin, the Father of Oregon. The first provisional governor of the Oregon country, George Abernethy, welcomed new arrivals from the Oregon Trail to the meadows on his property. Abernethy was a miller, who used the waterfalls of the Willamette to power his mills to grind flour. Men such as McLoughlin and Abernethy made Oregon City an early site of industry as well as the territory's first capital.

When Oregon gained statehood and expanded, the Willamette River became a main transportation highway. The falls at Oregon City were an obstacle because there the Willamette grew too shallow to allow large ships to pass. The capital was moved to Salem in 1851, and Portland became the state's major shipping location. Today, Oregon City is a small town with a population of 14,000 situated about 15 miles (24 km) south of Portland. ■

Few American landscapes are more spectacular than the Oregon coast. Rivers such as the Rogue, the Chetco, and the Gold cut through the slopes of the Coast Range, emptying into the ocean. In those areas, boaters, fishing enthusiasts, and nature lovers find a wilderness paradise.

Oregon's residents have long cherished their seashore. Efforts have been made to limit its purchase by individuals. As a result, more than two-thirds of the Oregon coast is open to the public.

Visitors to the coast can choose from a wide variety of activities. Several national forests offer recreational activities such as hiking, fishing, and strolling along the beach.

In the town of Newport, visitors to the Oregon Coast Aquarium can see an enormous variety of sea life from jellyfish to sea lions. Sea lions can also be viewed up close near Florence at the Sea Lion Caves—the world's largest sea caves—where an elevator takes visitors 1 mile (1.6 km) down cliffside to view the sea lions up close. History buffs can choose from several historical museums

The Oregon coast provides a home for sea lions.

that display relics from early Native Americans to aircraft from World War II.

The Cascade Range

The majestic Cascades run north to south the entire length of Oregon. Within this range lie two of the most extraordinary sights in America. The first, the most recognizable landmark in the state, is Mount Hood. It towers over Portland in the north. The mountain draws more hikers and climbers to its snowcapped summit each year than any other mountain in North America. And annually, more than 5,000 climbers attempt to scale the peak. Although Mount Hood is not steep, climbing it is not without risk. Shifting

Crater Lake (left) is the deepest lake in the United States.

Mount Hood is a challenge for even the most seasoned climbers.

The Banana Belt

Although the climate is cool and moist along most of Oregon's coast, an area known as the Banana Belt is warm enough to grow tropical plants such as lemon trees and banana palms. The Banana Belt, which lies on the Chetco River near the town of Brookings, is sheltered by a large shoulder of land that keeps away the constant, chilling winds. This steep shoulder of land also makes the mouth of the Chetco one of the calmest and safest of the eleven harbors along the coast, a favorite among small-boat owners who take to its smooth waters for a day of fishing. The Banana Belt is the fastest-growing area of the state. ■

A hillside of Indian paintbrush below Mount Jefferson

snow packs and unpredictable storms can cause sudden danger. In fact, five climbers died in an avalanche in the 1980s.

The second unusual attraction is Crater Lake, Oregon's only national park, at the southern end of the Cascades. Created more than 7,000 years ago when the top of a volcano exploded, the crater filled with water from surrounding glaciers, forming the deepest lake in the United States. Tourists from around the world come to the park each year to view Crater Lake's astonishing blue waters against the beauty of its natural surroundings.

The Cascades are a chain of extinct and inactive volcanoes that jut skyward in jagged peaks. In addition to Mount Hood, the largest include Mount Jefferson, a 10,500-foot (3,202-m) peak in central

Oregon, and the nearby Three Sisters, extinct volcanoes towering more than 10,000 feet (3,050 m) high.

There are few towns here, but there is no shortage of people. Ski resorts, logging camps, and sanctuaries set aside for nature lovers bring thousands of people to these mountains.

The ease with which people can hike, bike, ski, snowmobile, and log in the Cascades has led to concerns that the area's plant and animal life are threatened. In recent years, the U.S. Forest Service has proposed limits on land use near Mount Hood. Overuse and careless campers have damaged the area, according to officials.

Multnomah Falls in the Columbia River Gorge National Scenic Area is the highest waterfall in the state.

Hood River and the Columbia River Gorge

Northeast of Mount Hood, the Hood River winds its way toward the Columbia River. Where the Hood flows into the deep gorge cut by the river at that point, powerful winds create perfect conditions for windsurfers.

Rounding up cattle in an Oregon winter

High Desert Country

On the eastern side of the Cascade Range is the region known as the Columbia Plateau or the high desert country. Although they are not as populated as areas west of the Cascades, towns on the plateau, such as Baker City, La Grande, and Pendleton, have the flavor of the Old West.

Cattle ranching once played a large part in the economy of this area. Today, wheat, wool, and lumber are the major industries, but those who grew up raising cattle do their jobs as they have done them for generations. Cowboys who live in the high desert still rope, brand, and herd cattle. And every September, cowhands from all corners of the United States and Canada are welcomed to the Pendleton Round-Up, America's oldest and largest rodeo.

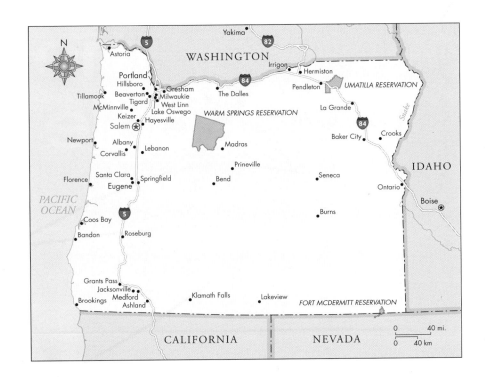

Oregon's cities and interstates

Pendleton Underground

Pendleton has always been known as a Wild West town. In the 1870s, laborers arrived from China to help build the railroads that connected the West and East.

In those days, Chinese immigrants suffered from extreme prejudice—some of the toughest anti-immigration laws in U.S. history were passed to keep Chinese people out. In Pendleton, a local law prohibited Chinese from living in town or owning property there. But the Chinese immigrants got around that law by living *under* Pendleton.

From the 1870s until the 1900s, Chinese immigrants dug more than 70 miles (113 km) of tunnels under Pendleton. A whole community was created with living areas, stores, restaurants, and laundries. When Pendleton was nearly destroyed by a flood in 1882, other settlers decided that the tunnels were a good idea and they too set up businesses there. ■

CHAPTER SEVEN

For the People

Oregon entered the Union as the thirty-third state on February 14, 1859—Valentine's Day. Seeing no reason to invent a new type of state government, Oregonians followed the model of government drawn up by the founders of the United States. Oregon's voters (only white males were allowed to vote at the time) had already approved the state constitution in 1857.

Today, all U.S. citizens and Oregon residents eighteen years of age and older are eligible to vote in national and state elections. The Oregon constitution, like the U.S. Constitution, divides the government into three branches: executive, legislative, and judicial.

Executive Branch

Every four years, Oregonians elect a governor, secretary of state, treasurer, attorney general, commissioner of labor and industries, and superintendent of public instruction. These six elected officials

Opposite: The capitol in Salem

**Governor John
Kitzhaber**

make up the executive branch of the state government. Each official manages a state agency or commission.

As the chief administrator, the governor serves on several state boards and is the chairman of the land-use board. It is the governor's responsibility to submit a budget to the legislature every two years. All bills passed by the legislature are either signed into law or vetoed by the governor.

Oregon's governor is limited to a maximum of two four-year terms within a twelve-year period. The state has no lieutenant governor. If the governor is unable to complete a term, it is served by the secretary of state.

Legislative Branch

The legislature of Oregon is divided into a senate and a house of representatives. Oregon's senate has thirty members who are

**The Oregon senate
chamber**

Oregon's Governors

Name	Party	Term	Name	Party	Term
John Whiteaker	Dem.	1859–1862	A. W. Norblad	Rep.	1929–1931
A. C. Gibbs	Rep.	1862–1866	Julius L. Meier	Ind.	1931–1935
George L. Woods	Rep.	1866–1870	Charles H. Martin	Dem.	1935–1939
La Fayette Grover	Dem.	1870–1877	Charles A. Sprague	Rep.	1939–1943
Stephen F. Chadwick	Dem.	1877–1878	Earl Snell	Rep.	1943–1947
W. W. Thayer	Dem.	1878–1882	John H. Hall	Rep.	1947–1949
Z. F. Moody	Rep.	1882–1887	Douglas McKay	Rep.	1949–1952
Sylvester Pennoyer	Dem.-Pop.	1887–1895	Paul L. Patterson	Rep.	1952–1956
William Paine Lord	Rep.	1895–1899	Elmo Smith	Rep.	1956–1957
T. T. Geer	Rep.	1899–1903	Robert D. Holmes	Dem.	1957–1959
George E. Chamberlain	Dem.	1903–1909	Mark O. Hatfield	Rep.	1959–1967
Frank W. Benson	Rep.	1909–1910	Tom McCall	Rep.	1967–1975
Jay Bowerman	Rep.	1910–1911	Robert W. Straub	Dem.	1975–1979
Oswald West	Dem.	1911–1915	Victor G. Atiyeh	Rep.	1979–1987
James Withycombe	Rep.	1915–1919	Neil Goldschmidt	Dem.	1987–1991
Ben W. Olcott	Rep.	1919–1923	Barbara Roberts	Dem.	1991–1995
Walter M. Pierce	Dem.	1923–1927	John Kitzhaber	Dem.	1995–
I. L. Patterson	Rep.	1927–1929			

elected to four-year terms. Its house of representatives has sixty members who are elected for two years. The legislature meets in January of odd-numbered years.

The legislature's main responsibilities are to finance state government, pass laws, and provide sessions for open discussion of public issues and concerns. The legislature also reviews the state budget. It passes tax laws to provide funds for state agencies. Any bills passed by the legislature that are vetoed by the governor can be signed into law with a two-thirds majority.

Wayne Morse, Independent Thinker

Wayne Morse was a college professor at the University of Oregon in 1944 when he was elected to the U.S. Senate as a Republican. He said many times that the most important question he asked himself before any Senate vote was "What do the facts show the best public interest to be?"

Morse was widely respected for his intelligence and independent spirit. In the 1950s he supported civil rights for African-Americans, an unpopular stand at that time. He also supported labor rights for workers, another controversial stand. His opposition to the western land-use policies of President Dwight D. Eisenhower, a Republican, led Morse to switch parties, and he became a Democrat in 1955. A year later, Republicans swept into power behind Eisenhower, but Oregon voters sent Wayne Morse back to the Senate—a sign of their respect for his independence.

Morse became most well known in the early 1960s for his opposition to U.S. intervention in Vietnam. A strong believer in nonviolence and in the proper role of the United Nations as a world force for peace, Morse felt that the leaders of the U.S. government were violating the concepts of the United Nations. Although there was no formal declaration of war, U.S. senators were asked to approve the use of military forces in Vietnam. In a speech opposing the use of U.S. troops, Morse said "In Vietnam, we have broken the United Nations charter . . . this does our country great damage around the world."

Wayne Morse was one of only two senators out of one hundred to oppose sending U.S. forces to Vietnam. His vote cost him his Senate seat in 1968, even though his beliefs about the war were proved to be correct. Morse died in 1974 while campaigning to regain his Senate seat. ■

Judicial Branch

As is the case with the federal government's judicial branch, the state supreme court directs Oregon's judicial system. However, while the U.S. Supreme Court's nine justices are appointed for life, the Oregon supreme court has seven justices elected for six-year terms. It is the responsibility of the judicial branch to interpret and rule on the legality of actions taken by the legislature and by state agencies of the executive branch. The supreme court also hands down decisions on civil, criminal, and governing cases. Below the supreme court, the judicial branch includes an appeals court, as well as circuit, district, county, and municipal courts.

Oregon's counties

The Oregon System

Oregon's wealth of natural resources and economic opportunities led to one of the most important reforms in American politics. By the late 1800s, a number of very wealthy and powerful men controlled the state. Some of these people ran the railroads and the shipping industries. Others served in the state government and often listened more closely to the wealthy than to the workers and farmers who made up the majority.

By the turn of the century, charges of election fraud were heard throughout the state. Lawmakers' votes were being bought by rich businessmen.

However, a man named William U'Ren (above, right) would soon change the shape of Oregon politics. He saw that a few wealthy people controlled the state capital and the railroads, forests, and waterways in the rest of the state. He proposed an amendment to the state constitution that would allow initiative and referendum.

An initiative allows voters to propose laws. Previously, only elected representatives could propose laws. And a referendum

allows all citizens to vote on the legislation, instead of permitting only elected representatives to pass bills.

The amendment to Oregon's constitution allowing what is known as direct legislation was passed in 1902. Many reforms followed. Public officials could now be voted out of office. Laws regulating work hours and workplace safety were passed. Laws forbidding child labor and requiring equal job opportunities for women were also passed.

These new ideas in politics became known as the Oregon System and are common in many states today. In recent years, voters in Oregon have used their system to keep state lands from being developed and to create strict environmental laws. ■

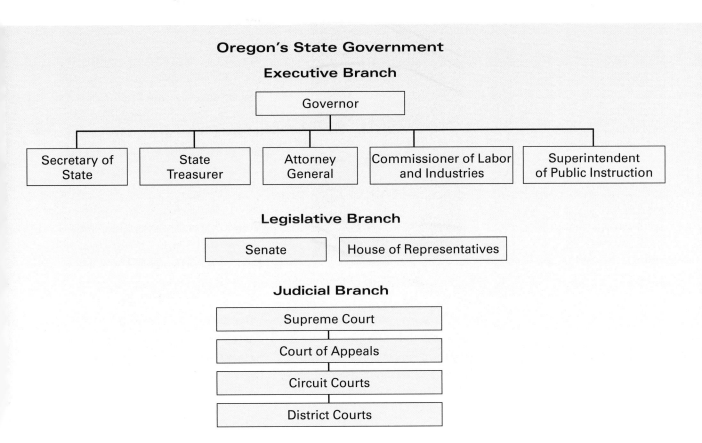

Oregon's State Government

Executive Branch

Governor

| Secretary of State | State Treasurer | Attorney General | Commissioner of Labor and Industries | Superintendent of Public Instruction |

Legislative Branch

Senate | House of Representatives

Judicial Branch

Supreme Court

Court of Appeals

Circuit Courts

District Courts

Local Government

An administrative body known as a county commission controls most of Oregon's thirty-six counties. Commissions have three to five members who are elected for four-year terms. Eight counties are run by a system known as home rule, which allows them to choose any form of government they wish.

The same home rule is used in most of Oregon's communities. Most large cities are governed by a council and a manager. Portland, the largest city, has a mayor and four commissioners.

Oregon's State Flag and Seal

The state seal (bottom) is a shield with the American eagle. Below the shield are thirty-three stars—signifying that Oregon was the thirty-third state admitted to the Union—and a ribbon carrying the inscription *The Union*. Above the ribbon are scenes that represent Oregon history. The mountains and forests of Oregon against the sun setting over the Pacific Ocean provide a background for an ox-drawn wagon, an elk, a departing British warship, and an arriving American merchant ship. Below the ribbon, a sheaf of wheat, a plow, and a miner's pick symbolize Oregon's resources and industries.

The state flag (left, top) has a field of navy blue with the state seal in gold, which appears above the year—1859—when Oregon became a state. The flag was officially adopted in 1925. The reverse side of the flag shows a beaver, the state animal. ■

Oregon's State Song
"Oregon, My Oregon"

Words by J. A. Buchanan   Music by Henry B. Murtagh

Land of the empire builders, land of the golden west;
Conquered and held by free men, fairest and the best.
Onward and upward ever, forward and on and on;
Hail to thee, land of heroes, my Oregon.

Land of the rose and sunshine, land of the summer's breeze;
Laden with health and vigor, fresh from Western seas.
Blest by the blood of martyrs, land of the setting sun;
Hail to thee, land of Promise; my Oregon.

Oregon's State Symbols

State mammal: Beaver The beaver was named the state mammal in 1969. The fur of the beaver brought the first Europeans to the state. Once hunted nearly to extinction, the largest of North America's rodents can now be seen building dams in the state's waterways.

State bird: Western meadowlark (top, right) This brown spotted bird can be seen swooping through fields at dusk capturing insects for food. A poll of schoolchildren in 1927 led to the designation of this beloved songbird as the state bird.

State fish: Chinook salmon The largest of the Pacific salmon, this fish sustained Native American tribes for centuries. Adopted as the state fish in 1961, the chinook provides a livelihood for many Oregonians in the fishing industry.

State insect: Oregon swallowtail butterfly This bright butterfly became the state insect in 1979. In late summer, the sagebrush canyons of the Columbia River and its tributaries are an explosion of orange as the swallowtails emerge.

State flower: Oregon grape (bottom, right) The mild weather of the Pacific Coast provides a perfect environment for the Oregon grape. The plant's green hollylike leaves and bright yellow flowers are easily recognized along coastal highways.

State gemstone: Oregon sunstone The large, brightly colored stone is a member of the feldspar family. It is found mainly in the deserts of southeastern Oregon.

State rock: Thunderegg Also known as geodes, these rocks contain many minerals. Cutting them open reveals wonderful designs of multicolored crystals that can be cut and polished.

State nut: Hazelnut The hazelnut was named the state nut in 1989. Oregon grows 99 percent of all hazelnuts produced in the United States.

State tree: Douglas fir The slopes of the Coast Range and the Cascades are covered with this majestic evergreen. Declared the state tree in 1939, the Douglas fir is the source of most of Oregon's softwood lumber production.

State seashell: Oregon hairy triton Adopted in 1991, this shell—formally known as *Fusitriton oregonensis*—is found on beaches along the coast. Named for Oregon Territory, it is the only shell that bears a state's name.

CHAPTER EIGHT

Earning a Living in Oregon

The first white men to explore Oregon came for one thing—animal fur. Beaver and otter skins took the place of money for mountain men and traders. The word *buck*, meaning one dollar, comes from *buckskin*—the skin of the deer used to make clothing and footwear in the Old West.

A field of cabbage, pumpkin, and ornamental shrubs in Multnomah County

However, the days of fur trapping and trading were only a memory by the time the wagon trains began to roll across the Oregon Trail. The first settlers to arrive in Oregon in the 1840s were farmers. They built farms in the fertile Willamette Valley, where the newcomers grew wheat and produced dairy products.

The seemingly endless green forests that carpeted much of the state were perfect for loggers. As more people came to the state, more houses were needed, and the timber industry began to thrive.

Fish were the third natural resource that created jobs and built Oregon's early economy. The salmon that swam upstream each year to spawn had been a major food source for Native Americans and early traders. Once canning and refrigeration were invented, they became a cash product.

The main problem Oregon's economy faced during its first fifty years was transportation of goods. Railroads connecting the state with eastern states were not completed until the late nineteenth century. The Columbia River could be navigated by cargo

Opposite: The logging industry

ships only as far east as Portland, which left most of the areas east of the Cascades without transportation since the river was filled with rapids at that time.

Today, much of Oregon's economy is still based on its plentiful natural resources. But, as the state approaches its 150th anniversary, the economy has also undergone important changes.

Manufacturing

Today, more than 20 percent of Oregon's jobs are in technology and manufacturing, instead of timber and agriculture. At one time, even manufacturing jobs were tied to the timber industry. More than 60 percent of such jobs were in the manufacture of cardboard, plywood, and similar products. Now, manufacturing jobs are spread across many industries, which provides a more dependable economy.

The fastest-growing area is high technology. Oregonians make software, electronic measurement devices, computers, and other

Pendleton Woolen Mills

Recycled Shoes

As a teenager in the 1970s, Julie Lewis developed a deep love for Oregon. She took the message of saving the environment and recycling very seriously—so seriously that she is now the vice president of a shoe company called Deja.

Deja, based in Portland, sells shoes designed by Lewis. They are sturdy hiking shoes with a cotton canvas top woven from recycled textiles. The foam padding inside the shoes is made from discarded furniture cushioning. And other parts of the shoes are made from file folders, recycled paper bags, tires, and plastic wrap.

Deja ships out more than 100,000 shoes each year. What happens when the shoes wear out? "You can send them back to us to be recycled," says Lewis. ■

Just Do It

In 1957, high school runner Phil Knight (right) decided to attend the University of Oregon in Eugene, where he trained under Bill Bowerman, one of the top track coaches in the United States. When Knight left Oregon with a graduate degree in business, he decided to combine business with pleasure by selling imported running shoes. Bowerman joined a new company called Blue Ribbon Sports, helping with the design of running shoes.

One morning in 1971, Bowerman was eating waffles and staring at a waffle iron when he hit upon an idea for a new type of sole for a running shoe. He poured liquid rubber into the waffle iron and created a running shoe that provided a better grip on running surfaces.

In 1972, that running shoe with the now-famous swish logo went on the market. Knight and Bowerman changed the name of their company to Nike, for the Greek goddess of victory. By 1979, Nike controlled 50 percent of the running-shoe industry. And they continue to grow, using athletes such as Michael Jordan to represent their products.

In 1996, Nike Inc., based in Beaverton, made more than $6.5 billion. Although the company employs about 2,400 Oregonians, Nike shoes are made in Asia where wages are lower. Knight has been criticized by some who feel that the company is taking advantage of foreign workers. Nike, however, argues that it has recently instituted new policies regarding hours, wages, and safety in its overseas plants. ■

electronic equipment. Most high-technology companies are found in the greater Portland area, but some are now located in southern Oregon and east of the Cascades.

Forestry

Oregon's total land area is slightly more than 60 million acres (24.3 million ha). Of that, almost 28 million acres (11.3 million ha) is forested land. Oregon has been the largest producer of lumber in the United States since 1938. About one-sixth of the softwood lumber produced in the United States comes from Oregon.

**Logs prepared for
shipment in Astoria**

Forestry and related industries such as production of lumber, paper, plywood, and furniture provide almost one-third of the jobs in the state. As important as forestry has been to the state, however, the number of trees cut over the past twenty-five years has declined because of government regulations. More than 50 percent of Oregon's forests are on federally owned land. Laws protecting certain species such as the northern spotted owl, as well as strict antipollution and replanting requirements, have kept loggers out of government land.

Much of the timber from Oregon is cut on land that is privately owned by lumber companies. However, as more people move to Oregon, less private forestland is available to logging companies. Housing is taking over places that once might have supplied timber to be shipped out of state.

What Oregon Grows, Manufactures, and Mines

Agriculture and Fishing	Manufacturing	Mining
Timber	Wood products	Sand and gravel
Greenhouse and nursery products	Electric equipment	Stone
Beef cattle	Food products	Pumice
Milk	Machinery	Clays
Wheat	Paper products	Gold
	Scientific instruments	Semiprecious gems
	Printed materials	

Hazelnut-stuffed Pears

This scrumptious dessert features two Oregon specialties: pears and hazelnuts.

Ingredients:

   6 medium ripe pears, peeled, halved, and cored

1½ cups water

1/3 cup white grape juice

1/2 cup finely chopped hazelnuts

  2 tablespoons brown sugar

1/8 teaspoon vanilla extract

Directions:

Place pears flat side down in an ungreased 13"x 9"x 2" baking dish.

In a bowl, combine the water and grape juice, then pour over the pears. Cover the dish and bake at 350°F in a preheated oven for 35 to 45 minutes or until pears are tender. Remove from oven and turn the pears over.

Mix together the hazelnuts, sugar, and vanilla extract. Spoon into the pear cavities. Bake uncovered for another 5 minutes.

Serves 6.

Agriculture

Agriculture has been at the heart of Oregon's economy for more than a century. Today, there are about 60,000 farmworkers in Oregon. Adding those who work in the transportation, storage, and processing of agricultural goods brings the total to about 140,000—about 18 percent of the state's workers.

The key to Oregon's agricultural success is that the crops are so

A rainbow created from a corn crop's irrigation spray

varied. Oregon is the number-one producer of Christmas trees, grass seed, hazelnuts, peppermint, raspberries, and blackberries in the United States. It is also a major producer of plums, onions, cauliflower, and pears.

More than 80 percent of Oregon's agricultural products go out of state. Half of that amount goes to other countries, mainly Japan, South Korea, the Philippines, and Saudi Arabia. Greenhouse and nursery products, beef cattle, milk, and wheat are some of the state's most valuable products.

With more than 200 products, Oregon's agriculture has a wide variety of customers. However, agriculture, like forestry, faces problems as the state's population continues to grow. The first concern is land. Seventy percent of the best farmland is found in the Willamette Valley, but the valley has experienced large population growth and development since the 1980s. Much of the best land has been converted to industrial or residential use.

Water is another concern for the agriculture industry. Almost half of all farms in Oregon depend on irrigation from state waterways. However, a growing population needs water just as it needs land, and the supply is limited. Many waterways are also needed to support the fish population for commercial and recreational use.

Piloting the Big Ships

For more than a century, Portland has been the major shipping port for Oregon's agricultural goods. Today, more than 60 percent of all goods shipped from Portland are agricultural in nature. And the Columbia River system is the second-busiest river shipping system in the nation, after the Mississippi.

But shipping goods from Portland 100 miles (161 km) down the Columbia River to the Pacific Ocean is not as simple as just pointing the boat in the right direction. At the mouth of the river, where it flows into the ocean, the power of the water is awesome. The irresistible flow of a 1,200-mile (1,930-km) river colliding with mighty ocean tides can spin a 1,000-foot (305-m) supertanker around as if it were a toy boat. Through the years, at least 2,000 ships, have been wrecked in the turbulent waters and more than 1,500 lives have been lost.

This is why all ships arriving in or leaving from Portland must have a Columbia River pilot at the wheel. No ship captain is allowed to navigate the 100-mile (161-km) stretch between the Pacific and Portland.

Along the twists and turns of the Columbia, pilots may change course a hundred times during one trip. Fog rolling in can cause complete blindness. Pilots may be required to navigate the river without seeing the shoreline once. Fortunately, most know the river's ways by heart. To make things even tighter, the channel for the largest ships is just 600 feet (183 m) wide, so pilots must be extra careful when they meet oncoming traffic.

"The best way to pass another ship is to steer straight at it, then veer off at the last minute," says Captain Mitch Boyce, one of only fifty Columbia River pilots. ■

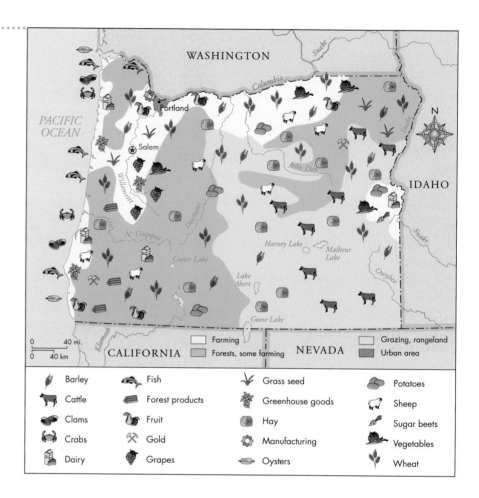

Oregon's natural resources

Map legend:

Map area types:
- Farming
- Forests, some farming
- Grazing, rangeland
- Urban area

Resources:
- Barley
- Cattle
- Clams
- Crabs
- Dairy
- Fish
- Forest products
- Fruit
- Gold
- Grapes
- Grass seed
- Greenhouse goods
- Hay
- Manufacturing
- Oysters
- Potatoes
- Sheep
- Sugar beets
- Vegetables
- Wheat

Fish and Wildlife

Oregon's abundant natural resources include a variety of fish and wildlife. The commercial and recreational sides of this economic sector bring in more than $1 billion for Oregon's residents every year. The money goes to small businesses, commercial fishers, charter-boat owners, tourist operators, and food processors.

One of Oregon's first industries was commercial fishing. The harvests from the ocean and rivers helped develop the state's economy and establish cities and ports in the early years.

For most of the state's history, the main catch has been chinook

Fishing boats in the
Newport harbor

and coho salmon. During the early 1990s, however, years of over-fishing led to a severe shortage of salmon, so limits were placed on catches. The chinook salmon population grew for several years and the limits were eased. But the coho salmon has remained at historically low levels and is close to becoming an endangered species.

Today, the biggest market for commercial fishers in Oregon is found in Pacific bottom-dwelling "groundfish" such as snapper, sole, and whiting. Harvest of these fish increased from 5 million pounds (2.3 million kg) in 1990 to 155 million pounds (70.4 million kg) in 1996.

Sport fishing also plays an important role in the state's economy. With more than 62,000 miles (99,758 km) of fishing streams, and 6,000 lakes and reservoirs, year-round fishing is almost always available. Small businesses selling licenses and other fishing needs serve more than 700,000 fishing enthusiasts each year.

Hunting also brings income into the state as more than 300,000 hunters buy licenses and supplies each year. The state operates sixteen wildlife hunting areas, and much of the money spent on hunting helps remote and economically depressed areas.

Tourism

One of the newest parts of Oregon's economy is tourism. Since the days of the fur traders, the beauty of Oregon has been well known. But the completion of interstate highways in the 1950s allowed tourists easy access to Oregon from all over the United States. In the 1990s, tourism increased by 36 percent and, by 1996, visitors brought in about $4.5 billion a year.

Tourism is important in several ways. It provides large numbers of entry-level jobs for younger workers. It offers more experienced workers the opportunity to work in management. In addition to jobs directly connected to tourism, other businesses such as retail sales, insurance, and real estate benefit from increased tourism.

Besides its almost countless number of natural sites for visitors to enjoy, Oregon's man-made attractions also draw visitors—and provide jobs. The Oregon Coast Aquarium, the End of the Oregon Trail Interpretive Center, the Oregon Museum of Science and Industry, and other spots all draw appreciative crowds.

As with other aspects of the state's economy, the growing tourist industry has caused some concern. Overuse of many natural areas has endangered plant- and wildlife. Arguments over the ways

that land is used, such as by snowmobilers, cross-country skiers, jet skiers, and rafters, has led to conflict. Many Oregon residents worry that too many tourists could damage the natural beauty they have come to enjoy.

This cruise boat in Cascade Locks is just one of the attractions for tourists in Oregon.

CHAPTER NINE

Who Lives in Oregon?

I f you were to meet a group of young people from Portland or Pendleton, chances are it would be difficult to call any one of them a typical Oregonian. They might include a boy whose ancestors came to the state on the Oregon Trail in the 1840s. There might be a girl whose ancestors came from China to help build the state's railroads in the 1880s or from Japan to farm. There might be someone whose ancestors came from Europe to build roads. There might be an African-American whose ancestors worked on the railroads, a Mexican American whose ancestors farmed, or a Native American whose ancestors were the first people of Oregon.

Although Oregon is overwhelmingly white, more and more ethnically diverse people are moving to the state.

Oregonians, like all Americans, are a mixture of the histories and traditions that make the nation unique. For the first arrivals, opportunity was found in fur-trapping and trading. These mountain men were mainly French, English, or Canadian.

The fur trade ended in the 1830s, but dreams of opportunity did not. In the 1830s, a number of Protestant missionaries came to Oregon. These were mainly American men of English descent who sought the opportunity to convert the Native Americans in Oregon to Christianity. Some of the first settlements in the Willamette Valley were church missions.

Opposite: A Portland powwow

The first wave of settlers came to Oregon during the 1840s. These people were Americans of English, German, and Scottish descent who farmed in the Willamette Valley. The first census in Oregon, taken in 1850, reported the population of the territory to be 12,093. By the time Oregon was a state, almost ten years later, the population was 52,465, showing that the number of white residents had increased more than 400 percent.

Other Races, Other Cultures

Until the Civil War, immigrants to Oregon were mainly white American-born people of English or northern European descent. Most of these immigrants made the journey to the state overland on the Oregon Trail. Because the state is so large and mountainous, the railroads did not reach Oregon until 1883, fourteen years after the first coast-to-coast railway connection was made in 1869. The hard work of building the railroads brought people from China, Italy, and Greece to Oregon. They were mostly young men who planned to earn as much money as possible before returning to their homeland. They were called "birds of passage."

Many of those who planned to leave Oregon never did. Instead they brought over families from their homelands or married other Oregonians and raised families. Large numbers of Chinese settled in Portland and east of the Cascades. They opened laundries, stores, and restaurants. During the late 1800s, prejudice forced Chinese immigrants to live together in separate areas of many communities called "Chinatowns."

Immigrants from southern European countries—mainly Italy and Greece—settled in the Portland area during the late 1800s.

A Chinese laundry in Salem in the early twentieth century

Jews fleeing anti-Semitic violence in eastern Europe settled in the Portland area at about the same time.

The arrival of railways brought African-Americans to Oregon. Prior to the Civil War, Oregon had passed the so-called Exclusion Law, which denied free blacks the right to live in Oregon. Although a small number of African-Americans had come to Oregon during the gold rush years of the late 1840s, most stayed away because of the law. After the Civil War, however, the Exclusion Law was ignored. One of the few occupations open to African-Americans was working on the railroads. As a result, a community of African-Americans, most employed by the railroad, grew up in Portland.

In the early 1900s, a number of Japanese immigrants arrived to work on small farms. Many eventually acquired their own land.

Between 1860 and 1910, the population of Oregon grew more than 1,000 percent from 52,465 to 672,765. The 1990 census counted 2,853,733 million people in Oregon. The government's latest population figures show the state has slightly more than 3 million people. Of those, whites make up 92.77 percent, Asians make up 2.44 percent, African-Americans make up 1.62 percent, Hispanic Americans make up 3.97 percent, and Native Americans make up 1.35 percent.

Crowds enjoying Waterfront Park in Portland

Where They Live

Oregon's population density of 29 people per square mile (11 per sq km) is very sparse when compared to smaller states on the East Coast. However, more than 70 percent of the people live in the Willamette Valley, and more than half the people live in the greater metropolitan Portland area. Much of the open land in the valley has been settled, and the problem of living space has become more important as the state's population continues to grow.

Religion

The first settlers in Oregon were mainly Protestants. Today the Protestant churches with the largest membership are Baptist, Lutheran, Methodist, Presbyterian, and Mormon. Roman Catholics are Oregon's largest

The First Presbyterian
Church in Jacksonville

religious group. One-sixth of the state's church members belongs
to Roman Catholic churches.

Education

Education has always played an important role in the life of Oregon's citizens. The state's educational system today spends more than the U.S. average on education, and the SAT scores of Oregon's high school students have consistently been among the nation's highest.

The first schools in Oregon's early days were founded by religious organizations. The first college in the Far West was Oregon Institute, founded in 1842 in Salem and later renamed Willamette University. Lewis and Clark College was founded in Portland in

Population of Oregon's Major Cities (1990)

Portland	437,319
Eugene	112,669
Salem	107,786
Gresham	68,235
Beaverton	53,310
Medford	46,951
Corvallis	44,757

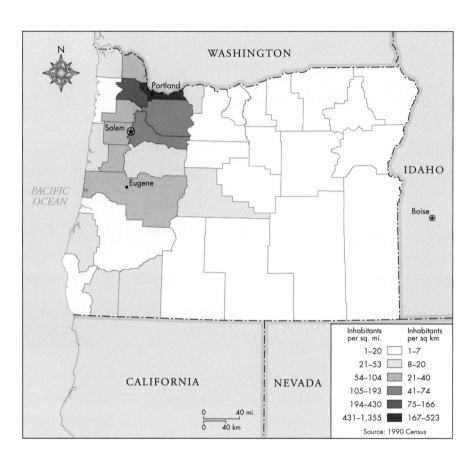

Oregon's population density

1867. The University of Portland, founded in 1901, is now the state's largest independent institution of higher learning.

Among Oregon's twenty-five public and twenty-six private institutions are the seven units of the Oregon university system. Oregon State University, founded in 1868 in Corvallis, and the University of Oregon, founded in 1872 in Eugene, are two nationally recognized institutions. Well-known private institutions include Reed College and Pacific Northwest College of Art in Portland, and Pacific University in Forest Grove.

Salem's Willamette University is Oregon's oldest college.

CHAPTER TEN

Lots to Do
and See

Canoeing is one way to appreciate the Mount Hood National Forest.

There's so much to do outdoors in Oregon that it's hard to imagine being indoors. Except that there's so much to do indoors too! Name your sport and you can play it or watch it in Oregon. Fishing, surfing, and clamming are just some of the activities people enjoy along the Oregon coast. Windsurfing, whitewater rafting, jet skiing, and kayaking are popular along the Columbia River as well as on the Willamette and Snake Rivers.

The state's thirteen national forests and 240 camping and recreational sites offer hiking, camping, and wildlife-viewing opportunities. In the Cascades of central Oregon, you can choose between skiing in the winter and mountain biking in the summer. Rock climbing and orienteering (a navigation competition) are also popular in the central Cascades.

Opposite: Climbing Smith Rock

In the eastern regions of Oregon, horseback riding, hunting, and fishing are among the most popular outdoor activities. The annual Pendleton Round-Up in September draws thousands of rodeo fans from around the country.

The Portland Trail Blazers have long been a powerful force in the NBA.

Spectator Sports

Few teams in any professional sport have as loyal a following as the Portland Trail Blazers of the National Basketball Association (NBA). The team began play in 1970 and won the NBA championship in 1978. That championship team was led by Bill Walton, perhaps the greatest athlete ever to play in the state. Walton, a dominating center, was Portland's "franchise player" for six years before moving on to other teams. He was inducted into the Basketball Hall of Fame and is now a nationally known television basketball analyst.

Before moving to the Rose Garden in 1995, the Trail Blazers played at the Portland Coliseum for twenty-five years. The team was so popular that they sold out all the seats in the coliseum for 810 straight games—a record unmatched in professional sports.

Other spectator sports that draw big crowds in the Portland area are minor-league baseball and hockey, as well as professional indoor soccer. The athletic teams of the largest state universities, the University of Oregon in Eugene and Oregon State University in Corvallis, also draw many spectators. The University of Oregon Ducks have a long and colorful football history. Many former Oregon players, such as Norm Van Brocklin, Dan Fouts, and Ahmad Rashad, went on to great acclaim in the National Football League. Track and field also has a long tradition at Oregon, and some of the greatest runners in the world are Oregon alumni, including Alberto Salazar, Steve Prefontaine, and Mary Decker Slaney.

Mary Decker Slaney

Mary Decker Slaney (right) has been in the world track spotlight since, at age fifteen, she set her first American record in the mile. In almost thirty years of running as Mary Decker—or under her married name Slaney—she has set seventeen world records and thirty U.S. records. She currently holds the U.S. records at 800, 1500, 2000, 3000 meters and the mile.

Slaney's career, for all its success, has been marked by misfortune. She has undergone more than twenty operations on her legs and feet due to overtraining and injuries. In the 3000 meter finals of the 1988 Olympics, Slaney was considered a favorite for a gold medal. Early in the race however, she was hemmed in by a pack of runners. Another runner's foot came up on the back of Mary's leg, sending her tumbling off the track and she was unable to complete the race. Now forty-two, Slaney continues to train in Eugene and competes in road races. ■

The Rose Garden

Portland is nicknamed the Rose City for the year-round blooming of the many varieties of that flower in the city. So it stands to reason that one of newest sports arenas in the country, which opened in 1995, would be called the Rose Garden.

The Garden is the home court of the Portland Trail Blazers and seats more than 21,000 people. The Garden is also used for college basketball, hockey, track and field, and gymnastics. Nonsports events such as monster truck rallies and rock concerts are also part of the Rose Garden schedule.

The ceiling of this cavernous arena is 140 feet (43 m) high. Slightly below ceiling level is a unique "acoustical cloud" comprised of 160 panels. The cloud can be moved to absorb noise—during a musical performance, for example. It can also be moved to reflect noise back down to the playing surface, making basketball games very loud. ■

Performing Arts in Southern Oregon

The natural beauty of southern Oregon, just north of the California border near Crater Lake, is well known. Two towns in the area host summer festivals. From July through Labor Day, Ashland is the scene of an annual Shakespeare festival. The works of the great playwright are performed in a replica of London's Globe Theatre. Summer performances of other dramatists are presented by nine other theater groups in Ashland.

About 15 miles (24 km) north of Ashland, the small town of Jacksonville hosts the Peter Britt Music Festival each August. Considered the premier music and performing arts event of the Northwest, the Britt Festival presents a wide range of musicians from folk singers to classical musicians.

Historic Jacksonville

During the 1850s, gold was discovered in the vicinity of the Rogue River, which flows through Jacksonville. Although nowhere near as rich as the California gold discovery, the Rogue River finding produced a small gold rush of its own. The town of Jacksonville was founded by early miners and merchants pursuing the precious metal—or the miners' money.

In 1966, the U.S. Department of the Interior designated Jacksonville a national historic landmark. The town's buildings are considered perfect examples of nineteenth-century mining and commercial architecture. Today more than eighty of Jacksonville's nineteenth-century stores, mills, and homes are listed in the National Register of Historic Buildings.

One house that is open to the public was the home of Jeremiah Nunan, built in 1893. This Queen Anne style building is known as the Catalogue House (above), because Nunan ordered the home from a catalogue as a Christmas present for his wife. It was shipped west from Knoxville, Tennessee, in fourteen boxcars. Assembly took six months. ■

Ashland is home to an annual Shakespeare festival and many other cultural events.

Libraries and Museums

Oregon's library system was one of the first west of the Rocky Mountains. The first library opened in Oregon City in 1834, before the first wave of pioneers had even crossed the Oregon Trail. Today, the state has about 200 libraries, with the largest in Portland. Because of the size of the state and the sparse population in some

The Beverly Cleary Children's Library is part of the Multnomah County Central Library.

areas, a state library bookmobile visits small communities on a regular basis. The state library also loans books by mail to remote areas. Each year Oregon's libraries loan out about nine books per resident, one of the highest rates in America.

The High Desert Museum

Just outside the town of Bend, on the eastern slopes of the Cascade Range, is one of the most popular museums in Oregon. The High Desert Museum is dedicated to the area, the history, and the culture of the huge dry plateau that makes up one-fourth of the state.

The museum houses scientific, Native American, literary, art, and historical collections. Walk-through dioramas provide realistic scenes of the desert peoples and pioneers. Outdoors, on the museum grounds, actual animals of the region, from birds of prey to porcupines, surround visitors. Built in the style of the Old West, the museum is open year-round. ■

There are a number of fine museums, many relating to the history of the Far West, throughout the state. Art museums are located in Portland and Eugene. Portland is also home to the Oregon Museum of Science and Industry as well as the museum and research library for the National Railway Historical Society.

John Reed was a native of Portland.

Two Famous Authors

In the early twentieth century, a Portland native named John Reed burst onto the scene with two firsthand accounts of revolutions in other countries. His book on the Mexican Revolution, *Insurgent Mexico*, was written in 1914 while Reed accompanied rebel leader Pancho Villa and his forces in their war against the Mexican government.

In 1917, Reed was in Russia for one of the most violent revolutions in history—the Communist overthrow of the Russian czar. His book of the first days of the fighting, *Ten Days That Shook the World,* was an international best-seller.

Reed, whose father was a U.S. marshal in Portland, was educated at Harvard University. After the Russian Revolution, Reed remained in Russia for several years. His work praising the Communists was not well received in the United States, and Reed was denied reentry to his own country. He died of typhus in Russia in 1920 at the age of thirty-three. A memorial to Reed, one of the founders of modern journalism, stands in Washington Park in Portland.

Another Oregon native and author who achieved fame for his writing—and notoriety for his lifestyle—is Ken Kesey. Kesey grew up in the Willamette Valley and graduated from Stanford University. In 1962, Kesey won national acclaim for his book *One Flew over the Cuckoo's Nest,* a story about inmates at a mental institution. Shortly after that book's release, Kesey and a group of people who called themselves the Merry Pranksters set off on a bus trip around the country. This journey, which occurred at the beginning of the hippie era in California, was described in a book called *The Electric Kool-Aid Acid Test* by journalist and novelist Tom Wolfe. Kesey is one of the main characters in the nonfiction account.

In 1964, Kesey published *Sometimes a Great Notion.* This novel told the story of the Stamper family and is a richly detailed story of the logging business set on the rugged coast of Oregon.

Today, Ken Kesey operates a farm in the Willamette Valley. Two of his books have been made into movies. *One Flew Over the Cuckoo's Nest*, starring Jack Nicholson, won several Academy Awards. *Sometimes a Great Notion* starred Henry Fonda, Paul Newman, and Lee Remick. Both movies were filmed in Oregon.

Ken Kesey grew up in Oregon and has based much of his writing in the state.

Timeline

United States History

The first permanent English settlement is established in North America at Jamestown.	**1607**
Pilgrims found Plymouth Colony, the second permanent English settlement.	**1620**
America declares its independence from Britain.	**1776**
The Treaty of Paris officially ends the Revolutionary War in America.	**1783**
The U.S. Constitution is written.	**1787**
The Louisiana Purchase almost doubles the size of the United States.	**1803**
The United States and Britain fight the War of 1812.	**1812–15**
The North and South fight each other in the American Civil War.	**1861–65**

Oregon State History

1579 Sir Francis Drake sails along the Oregon coast.

1792 Captain Robert Gray sails up the Columbia River and enters what is now Oregon.

1805 Lewis and Clark reach the Columbia River in October.

1811 Astoria is founded on the Columbia River by fur trader John Jacob Astor.

1813 In the War of 1812, British troops capture Astoria and rename it Fort George.

1818 As a result of the War of 1812, the United States and Britain agree that citizens of both nations can live in what is now Oregon.

1834 Nathaniel Wyeth, Hall Kelley, and a group of missionaries set out from Boston to settle more of Oregon, arriving in the Willamette Valley.

United States History

The United States is **1917–18**
involved in World War I.

The stock market crashes, **1929**
plunging the United States into
the Great Depression.

The United States **1941–45**
fights in World War II.
The United States becomes a **1945**
charter member of the U.N.

The United States **1951–53**
fights in the Korean War.

The U.S. Congress enacts a series of **1964**
groundbreaking civil rights laws.

The United States **1964–73**
engages in the Vietnam War.

The United States and other **1991**
nations fight the brief
Persian Gulf War against Iraq.

Oregon State History

1844 Slavery becomes illegal in Oregon,
and the brutal Lash Law is passed.

1848 Oregon Territory is officially created.

1850 The Oregon Donation Land Law goes
into effect.

1859 Oregon becomes the thirty-third state
on February 14.

1912 Women's suffrage is adopted in
Oregon.

1926 The Exclusion Law against African-
Americans is repealed.

1937 Bonneville Dam is completed.

1971 Oregon signs into law one of the
nation's first "bottle bills" banning
no-deposit beverage bottles.

1991 Barbara Roberts becomes Oregon's
first woman governor.

Fast Facts

Oregon state capitol

Statehood date	February 14, 1859, the 33rd state
Origin of state name	Although the origin is unknown, one theory holds that the name may have come from the French word *ouragan,* meaning "storm" or "hurricane."
State capital	Salem
State nickname	The Beaver State
State motto	"She flies with her own wings"
State bird	Western meadowlark
State flower	Oregon grape
State fish	Chinook salmon
State mammal	Beaver
State insect	Oregon swallowtail butterfly
State nut	Hazelnut
State song	"Oregon, My Oregon"
State tree	Douglas fir
State gemstone	Oregon sunstone

Western meadowlark

Oregon grape

State rock	Thunderegg
State seashell	Oregon hairy triton
State fair	Late August–early September at Salem
Total area; rank	97,131 sq. mi. (251,569 sq km); 10th
Land; rank	96,002 sq. mi. (248,645 sq km); 10th
Water; rank	1,129 sq. mi. (2,927 sq km); 26th
***Inland water;* rank**	1,049 sq. mi. (2,717 sq km); 19th
***Coastal water;* rank**	80 sq. mi. (207 sq km); 19th
Geographic center	Crook, 25 miles (40 km) southeast of Prineville
Latitude and longitude	Oregon is located approximately between 42° and 46° 18′ N and 116° 28′ and 124° 34′ W
Highest point	Mount Hood, 11,239 feet (3,428 m)
Lowest point	Sea level along the coastline
Largest city	Portland
Number of counties	36
Population; rank	2,853,733 (1990 census); 29th
Density	29 persons per sq. mi. (11 per sq km)
Population distribution	70% urban, 30% rural

Mount Hood

Ethnic distribution (does not equal 100%)		
	White	92.77%
	Hispanic	3.97%
	Asian and Pacific Islanders	2.44%
	Other	1.82%
	African-American	1.62%
	Native American	1.35%

Record high temperature	119°F (48°C) at Prineville on July 29, 1898, and at Pendleton on August 10, 1898
Record low temperature	–54°F (–48°C) at Ukiah on February 9, 1933, and at Seneca on February 10, 1933
Average July temperature	66°F (19°C)
Average January temperature	32°F (0°C)
Average annual precipitation	28 inches (71 cm)

Cape Kiwanda State Park

Natural Areas and Historic Sites

National Park

Crater Lake National Park, named for the deepest lake in the United States, was created by Mount Mazama, a volcano that collapsed more than 7,700 years ago. Visitors will enjoy driving around the rim of the lake as well as boating.

National Historical Park

Nez Perce National Historical Park encompasses thirty-eight different locations in Oregon and three other states. Its name honors the Nez Perce Indians, who originally lived there.

National Monuments and Memorials

The fossils in the John Day River Basin at *John Day Fossil Beds National Monument* date back 65 million years to the Cenozoic era.

Oregon Caves National Monument allows visitors to tour underground marble caves and hike through the above-ground old-growth forest that contains a fir tree with the largest circumference of any tree in the state.

A Douglas fir

Fort Clatsop National Memorial has a replica of the fort inhabited by Lewis and Clark during the winter of 1805, along with the saltworks used to make salt during their stay.

National Scenic Area

Columbia River Gorge National Scenic Area is an 8-mile (12.9-km)-long canyon that holds the Columbia River, cutting through the northwest's Cascade Range. It is home to more than 70,000 people.

National Forests

Oregon has thirteen national forests, scattered throughout the state. Southwest Oregon's Siskiyou National Forest, part of the Siskiyou Mountain Range extending into northern California, has the most diverse ecology in the Pacific Northwest. Each Christmas, families flock to Mount Hood National Forest to cut down pine trees. Umatilla National Forest in northeast Oregon is in the Blue Mountains and covers 1.4 million acres (567,00 ha).

State Parks

Oregon's state park system oversees more than 200 locations throughout the state, including trails, scenic viewpoints, and recreation sites. At Del Ray Beach State Recreation site, along the northwestern coast, visitors may enjoy a walk along the sands of the Pacific Ocean. In the southern region, Collier Memorial State Park displays antique logging equipment in a museum and features outstanding trout fishing. In the east, Kam Wah Chung State Heritage Site honors Chinese laborers.

Sports Teams

NCAA Teams (Division 1)
Oregon State University Beavers

University of Oregon Ducks

University of Portland Pilots

Trail Blazers

National Basketball Association
Portland Trail Blazers

Cultural Institutions

Libraries

The Oregon Historical Society Library in Portland has existed for 125 years. Its collections include pioneer memorabilia, Native American artwork, and other historical collections.

Oregon State University's *Valley Library* in Corvallis holds millions of books, microfilm, and government documents. The main library on campus includes collections on marine biology, entomology, and mathematics.

**Beverly Cleary
Children's Library**

The Salem Public Library has numerous events for adults and children, including the Discovery Room and Teen Scene area in its main branch.

Museums

The Portland Art Museum is the Pacific Northwest's oldest art museum. It holds more than 30,000 pieces of art in its permanent collection and also gives special exhibitions throughout the year.

The Oregon Coast Aquarium in Newport shows off its outdoor and indoor exhibits of water life from the state's coast.

The Oregon Museum of Science and Industry, south of downtown Portland, has an Omnimax theater as well as many exhibits for science enthusiasts.

The Museum of Natural History, at the University of Oregon in Eugene, displays artifacts from Oregon's natural and cultural past.

Performing Arts

Oregon has one major opera company, one major symphony orchestra, two major dance companies, and one professional theater company.

Willamette University

Universities and Colleges

In the mid-1990s, Oregon had twenty-five public and twenty-six private institutions of higher learning.

Annual Events

January–March

Sled Dog Races in Bend and Union Creek (January–February)

Seafood and Wine Festival in Newport (late February)

April–June

Pear Blossom Festival in Medford (mid-April)

All Northwest Barber Shop Ballad Contest and Gay Nineties Festival in Forest Grove (early May)

All-Indian Rodeo in Tygh Valley (mid-May)

Rhododendron Festival in Florence (mid-May)

Fleet of Flowers Memorial Service in Depoe Bay (late May)

Cannon Beach Sandcastle Contest in Cannon Beach (May)

Strawberry Festival in Lebanon (early June)

Rose Festival and parade in Portland (June)

Bach Summer Music Festival in Eugene (late June)

July–September

World Class Windsurfing in Hood River (July)

Butte to Butte 10K in Eugene (early July)

Rodeo in St. Paul (early July)

World Championship Timber Carnival in Albany (early July)

Buckeroo in Molalla (early July)

Chief Joseph Days in Joseph (late July)

Oregon Brewers Festival in Portland (late July)

Shakespeare Festival in Ashland (July–Labor Day)

Bigleaf and fine maples in fall

Big Wagon Days festival in Oregon City (August)

Regatta in Astoria (mid-August)

State fair in Salem (August–September)

Pendleton Round-Up (September)

Oktoberfest in Mount Angel (mid-September)

Cycle Oregon Bike Ride in different locations (September)

October–December

Lord's Acre Auction and Barbecue in Powell Butte (early November)

Kraut and Sausage Feed and Bazaar in Verboort (November)

Whale-watching on the coast (November–December)

Famous People

John Jacob Astor (1763–1848)	Financier and fur trader
Homer Davenport (1867–1912)	Cartoonist
Abigail Scott Duniway (1834–1915)	Teacher and women's rights leader
Eva Emery Dye (1855–1947)	Author
John Charles Frémont (1813–1890)	Explorer
Chief Joseph (1840?–1904)	Nez Perce leader
Ken Kesey (1935–)	Author
Joseph Lane (1801–1881)	Soldier and politician
Edwin Markham (1852–1940)	Poet
John McLoughlin (1784–1857)	Trapper and explorer
Thomas Lawson McCall (1913–1983)	Radio and television journalist and politician
Phyllis McGinley (1905–1978)	Teacher, poet, and essayist
Joseph Meek (1810–1875)	Trapper and pioneer

Ken Kesey

Brent Musburger (1939–)	Sportscaster
Linus Carl Pauling (1901–1994)	Chemist
John Reed (1887–1920)	Journalist and political radical
Eliza Hart Spalding (1807–1851)	Pioneer and missionary
Narcissa Prentiss Whitman (1808–1847)	Pioneer and missionary

To Find Out More

History

- Bratvold, Gretchen. *Oregon.* Minneapolis, MN: Lerner Publications Company, 1997.
- Fradin, Dennis Brindell. *Oregon.* Danbury, CT: Children's Press, 1995.
- Gregory, Kristiana. *Across the Wide and Lonesome Prairie: The Oregon Trail Diary of Hattie Campbell.* New York: Scholastic Trade, 1997.
- McAuliffe, Emily. *Oregon: Facts and Symbols.* Danbury, CT: Franklin Watts, 1999.
- Stein, Richard Conrad. *The Oregon Trail.* Danbury, CT: Children's Press, 1994.
- Thompson, Kathleen. *Oregon.* Austin, TX: Raintree/Steck Vaughn, 1996.
- Wills, Charles A. *A Historical Album of Oregon.* Brookfield, CT: Millbrook Press, 1995.

Fiction

- Jackson, Dave. *Attack in the Rye Grass.* Minneapolis, MN: Bethany House, 1994.
- Lawlor, Laurie. *American Sisters: West Along the Wagon Road 1852.* New York: Pocket Books, 1998.
- Van Leeuwen, Jean. *Bound for Oregon.* Illustrated by James Watling. New York: Dial Books for Young Readers, 1994.

Biographies

- Ludwig, Charles. *Jason Lee, Winner of the Northwest.* Illustrated by Charles Michael L. Denman. New York: Fromm International, 1993.
- Newton, David E. *Linus Pauling: Scientist and Advocate.* New York: Facts on File, Inc., 1994.

- Parkman, Francis, and Jane Shuter. *Francis Parkman and the Plains Indians*. Austin, TX: Raintree/Steck Vaughn, 1995.

Websites

- **Oregon Online**
  http://www.state.or.us
  Oregon's official website

- **Oregon Library Association**
  http://www.olaweb.org
  To find out about the state's libraries

- **Oregon Historical Society**
  http://www.ohs.org
  For information about the state's history and special exhibitions at the historical society

Addresses

- **Oregon Parks and Recreation Department**
  1115 Commercial Street NE
  Salem, OR 97310-1001
  To find out about the various state parks and recreational facilities in the state

- **Governor John A. Kitzhaber, M.D.**
  Oregon State Capitol
  Salem, OR 97310
  To find out about Oregon's state government

- **Portland Art Museum**
  1119 S.W. Park Avenue
  Portland, OR 97205
  For information on special exhibits and events

Index

Page numbers in *italics* indicate illustrations.

Meet the Author

Scott Ingram grew up in Connecticut. As a young graduate from the University of Connecticut, he lived and worked on the West Coast for two years. During that time, he visited a friend who lived just up the street from the Willamette River in Corvallis, Oregon. The beauty of the area stayed in his memory, and when the time came for Ingram to return to Connecticut, he made a point of driving across Oregon. The Willamette Valley was stunning as expected, but it was the high plateau on the east side of the Cascades that really surprised him.

"The high plains have a solitary beauty that I had never imagined. All I could think of was how it reminded me of the Old West. I never knew Oregon was such a big and diverse state," Ingram says. When the chance came along to write a book for Children's Press about a state he remembered fondly, he was more than happy to take on the task.

Ingram has spent most of working career writing for young people. A former managing editor for Weekly Reader Corporation, he wrote news articles, plays, and short stories for that company's classroom magazines for many years. He is the recipient of five Educational Press awards for his work and is also the author of several collections of short stories for young adults.

"I make my living as a writer, but reading history is a hobby of mine. That's another reason I decided to write this book; I was fascinated by Oregon's story," Ingram says. "For me, the past is alive. I like to imagine what places might have looked like before there were paved roads and power lines and malls."

Ingram enjoys spending hours in the local library investigating a topic and picking out interesting nuggets that will draw in readers. He has recently found the Internet to be a terrific resource for information.

"More and more organizations are setting up interesting and reliable websites that can be reached in seconds," says Ingram. "You can tour a museum. You can go to any community in a state. It can be a real time saver."

After the research and a detailed outline comes the writing. "There are no special tricks for that," says Ingram. "It's just roll up your sleeves and get busy." However, Ingram always keeps his readers foremost in his thoughts when he writes.

Ingram makes his home in a town with an "Oregonian" name—Portland, Connecticut—where he writes for educational publishers.

Photo Credits

Photographs ©:

AP/Wide World Photos: 119 (Al Behrman), 73 (Bob Galbraith), 54

Corbis-Bettmann: 118, 131 bottom (Agence France Presse), 42 (Michael Masian Historical Photographs), 47, 50 (Reuters), 109 (Joseph Sohm), 90, 124, 125, 134 bottom (UPI), 19, 35, 39, 40

Courtesy of the Governor's Office: 88 top

Dembinsky Photo Assoc.: 55 (Michael Hubrich), 6 bottom, 72 top (Anthony Mercieca)

Larry Geddis: cover, 8, 61, 67, 72 bottom, 74, 77 bottom, 79, 86, 87, 115, 122, 123, 128 top, 132, 133

Liaison Agency, Inc.: 99 (Evan Agostini)

New England Stock Photo: 9 (Marc A. Auth), 98 (Roger Bickel), 96 (Wayne Michael Lottinville), back cover (Jean Piggins)

North Wind Picture Archives: 37 (N. Carter), 10, 12, 15, 23, 26, 28, 44, 46, 51

Oregon Historical Society: 22 (OrHi 646), 29 (OrHi 53882), 31 (Or Hi59300), 32 right (Drawing by Oliver W. Dixon/OrHi1645), 33 (OrHi798), 34 (OrHi67763), 62 (OrHi49536), 92 (CN009663), 111 (0165G050)

Oregon Tourism Division: 94

Ric Ergenbright: 63, 80

Steve Terrill: 2, 6 top right, 6 top left, 6 top center, 7 top right, 56, 64, 68, 70, 76, 81 left, 82, 83, 95 bottom, 97, 102, 103, 108, 112, 121, 129 top, 131 top, 134 top

Stock Montage, Inc.: 14, 17, 18, 20, 21, 24, 32 left, 43, 52, 53

Superstock, Inc.: 78, 81 right, 88 bottom, 105, 107, 113, 117, 129 bottom

Tony Stone Images: 7 bottom, 84, 100 (Bruce Forster), 75 (Chuck Pefley), 59, 130 (Larry Ulrich), 65 (Greg Vaughn), 7 top left, 116 (Ted Wood)

Travel Stock: 57 (Buddy Mays)

Visuals Unlimited: 7 top center, 77 top (Bruce Berg), 95 top, 128 bottom (S. Maslowski)

Maps by XNR Productions, Inc.

The Life and World of

ELIZABETH I

Struan Reid

'IG 2014

www.heinemann/library.co.uk
Visit our website to find out more information about Heinemann Library books.

To order:
☎ Phone 44 (0) 1865 888066
🖺 Send a fax to 44 (0) 1865 314091
🖥 Visit the Heinemann Library Bookshop at www.heinemann/library.co.uk to browse our catalogue and order online.

First published in Great Britain by Heinemann Library,
Halley Court, Jordan Hill, Oxford
OX2 8EJ, part of Harcourt Education.
Heinemann is a registered trademark of Harcourt Education Ltd.

Editorial: Lucy Thunder and Helen Cox
Design: Ron Kamen and Celia Floyd
Illustrations: Jeff Edwards and Joanna Brooker
Picture Research: Rebecca Sodergren and Elaine Willis
Production: Séverine Ribierre

Originated by Ambassador Litho Ltd
Printed and bound in China by W K T

ISBN 0 431 14781 7 (hardback)
07 06 05 04 03
10 9 8 7 6 5 4 3 2 1

ISBN 0 431 14788 4 (paperback)
08 07 06 05 04
10 9 8 7 6 5 4 3 2 1

British Library Cataloguing in Publication Data
Reid, Struan
Life and world of Elizabeth I
942'.055'02

A full catalogue record for this book is available from the British Library.

Acknowledgements
The Publishers would like to thank the following for permission to reproduce photographs:
Bridgeman Art Library/Trustees of the National Museums & Galleries on Merseyside p. **4**; Bridgeman Art Library/Thyssen-Nomemisza Collection, Madrid, Spain p. **6**; Bridgeman Art Library/Hever Castle Ltd, Kent p. **7**; Bridgeman Art Library/Mark Fiennes, Loseley Park, Surrey p. **10**; Bridgeman Art Library/Prado Madrid, Spain p. **11**; Bridgeman Art Library/Hatfield House, Hertfordshire p. **12**; Bridgeman Art Library/National Portrait Gallery, London p. **13**; Bridgeman Art Library/Burghley House Collection, Lincolnshire p. **14**; Bridgeman Art Library/British Museum p. **15**; Bridgeman Art Library/Hermitage, St Petersburg p. **16**; Bridgeman Art Library/Mark Fiennes, Wollaton Hall, Nottingham p. **19**; Bridgeman Art Library/Scottish NAtional Portrait Gallery, Edinburgh p. **20**; Bridgeman Art Library/Castle Museum and Art Gallery, Nottingham p. **21**; Bridgeman Art Library/Victoria and Albert Museum p. **22**; Bridgeman Art Library/Society of Apothecaries, London p. **23**; Bridgeman Art Library/The Stapleton Collection p. **25**; Bridgeman Art Library/British Library p. **26**; Bridgeman Art Library/Fitzwilliam Museum, University of Cambridge p. **28**; Bridgeman Art Library/Private Collection p. **4**; Bridgeman Art Library/Roy Miles Fine Paintings p. **29**; British Library p. **24**; Hulton Getty p. **9**; Penhurst Place p. **17**; The Royal Collection © HM Queen Elizabeth II p. **8**; Topham Picturepoint p. **27**.

Cover photograph of Elizabeth I, reproduced with permission of the National Portrait Gallery.

The Publishers would like to thank Rebecca Vickers for her assistance in the preparation of this book.

Every effort has been made to contact copyright holders of any material reproduced in this book. Any omissions will be rectified in subsequent printings if notice is given to the Publishers.

Disclaimer
All the Internet addresses (URLs) given in this book were valid at the time of going to press. However, due to the dynamic nature of the Internet, some addresses may have changed, or sites may have changed or ceased to exist since publication. While the author and Publishers regret any inconvenience this may cause readers, no responsibility for any such changes can be accepted by either the author or the Publishers.

Contents

Any words appearing in the text in bold, **like this**, are explained in the Glossary.

Who was
Queen Elizabeth?

Elizabeth I was a brilliant and powerful queen who ruled England over 400 years ago. When she came to the throne in 1558, she **inherited** a deeply divided kingdom. For many years the people of England had been fighting each other over matters of religion. Queen Elizabeth was an extremely clever ruler and, by the time of her death nearly 50 years later, she had managed to unite her people. By then England had become one of the richest and most powerful countries in Europe.

▲ When she became queen, Elizabeth was always painted wearing the most magnificent clothes and jewels. In this way she showed herself to be a strong and powerful ruler.

A strong female ruler

Many people think that Elizabeth was the greatest English **monarch** who has ever reigned. She was the second daughter of King Henry VIII and the last member of the **Tudors**. The Tudor family was a royal **dynasty** that ruled England for more than a hundred years.

Elizabeth ruled her country at a time when most of the world's leaders were men, but she was as cunning and as quick as the best of them. She was much loved by her people and became known affectionately as Good Queen Bess.

How do we know?

We know a lot about Elizabeth I. Many portraits were painted of her and poems were written about her. Plays and music were composed for her by some of the most talented people of the day. These and many other sources, such as letters and government records, provide us with detailed information about the life and times of Elizabeth I – what she looked like and how she lived.

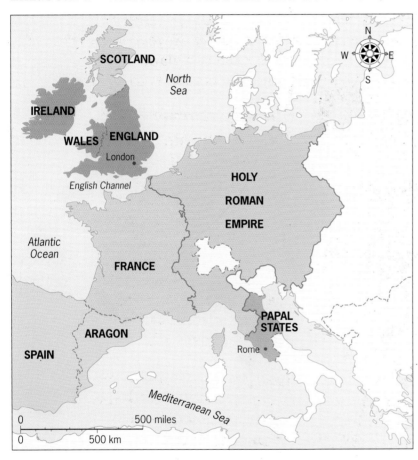

◀ This map shows the main kingdoms of Europe at the time Elizabeth I was born.

Key dates

1533	Henry VIII marries Anne Boleyn; Princess Elizabeth is born
1547	Henry VIII dies and Edward VI **succeeds** him
1553	Edward VI dies; Princess Mary becomes Queen Mary I
1558	Elizabeth becomes Queen of England when Mary I dies
1570	Elizabeth is **excommunicated** by the Pope
1588	The Spanish **Armada** is defeated
1603	Queen Elizabeth I dies

The birth of a princess

Elizabeth's father was King Henry VIII. He had already been ruling England for 24 years by the time Elizabeth was born. He was first married to a Spanish princess called Catherine of Aragon. She had given birth to a daughter, called Mary. At this time it was believed that kings were always much stronger and commanded more respect than queens. Henry longed to have a son who could **succeed** him, but Queen Catherine was now too old to have any more children.

A new wife

By now, Henry had fallen in love with a beautiful young lady at the royal court, called Anne Boleyn. He wanted to marry her and hoped that she would be able to give him the son he longed for. However, the Pope would not allow him to end his marriage to Catherine, so Henry decided to break with the **Catholic** Church in Rome. In 1534, he declared that he was now head of the Church in England. This meant he was now free to marry Anne. Although Henry refused to obey the Pope, he still kept his Catholic faith and did not become a **Protestant**.

▲ This portrait of Elizabeth's father, King Henry VIII, was painted by a famous German artist, called Hans Holbein. The king was proud of his looks and was a very good sportsman and musician as well as being a powerful king.

On 7 September 1533, at Greenwich Palace, the new Queen Anne gave birth to a princess, who was named Elizabeth. Henry was disappointed as he still had no son. The baby princess was born at one of the most important and exciting times in European history, when there were great religious upheavals that would change the world forever.

▶ Anne Boleyn, Elizabeth's mother. When she was a girl, Anne was sent away to be educated in France, where she learned to dress and behave in an elegant way. When she returned to England, she quickly caught the eye of King Henry VIII.

The Reformation

At this time, the Pope was head of the Roman Catholic Church and everyone, including kings, was supposed to obey everything he said. In 1517, a movement called the Reformation began. Some priests, such as Martin Luther, tried to reform or change certain things within the Roman Catholic Church. Their protests ended with the Christian Church splitting in two, with Catholics on one side and Protestants on the other. Roman Catholicism was eventually replaced in some countries by a new, reformed religion known as Protestantism.

A lonely childhood

Princess Elizabeth grew up away from the royal court. She saw very little of her parents and was looked after by nannies and nurses. Elizabeth was brought up as a **Protestant**. When aged only four, she began learning about **astronomy**, mathematics, history and geography. She also learned French and Italian. She was an extremely intelligent girl and read as many books as she could. Later, she learned Greek and Latin from her tutor. She could play musical instruments like the **virginals** and a guitar-like instrument called the lute. Elizabeth was also a very good dancer.

Terror at court

Princess Elizabeth's mother, Anne Boleyn, was in great danger. She had still not given birth to a baby boy and King Henry was beginning to spend more of his time with a lady-in-waiting called Jane Seymour.

▼ A portrait of Elizabeth aged 13. She is shown with books, and was one of the most educated women of her day.

Henry started plotting against Queen Anne. She was accused of all sorts of terrible crimes, including having love affairs with other men behind the king's back. On 19 May 1536, Anne was **executed** at the Tower of London. Elizabeth, who was less than three years old when her mother died, probably did not really know what had happened. She was still so young and had seen so little of her mother ever since she was born.

Elizabeth's stepmothers

A few days after Anne Boleyn's execution, King Henry married Jane Seymour and both Elizabeth and her half-sister Mary were declared **illegitimate**. This was a very dangerous time for the two princesses and Elizabeth soon learned to keep quiet so as not to attract attention.

In 1537, Jane Seymour gave birth to the longed-for son and heir, who was named Edward, but she died soon afterwards. Henry married three more times and so Elizabeth had three more stepmothers: Anne of Cleves, whom Henry just as quickly divorced; Catherine Howard, who, like her cousin Anne Boleyn, was executed; and finally Catherine Parr, who managed to outlive the king.

▲ This engraving shows Elizabeth being taught by her tutor Roger Ascham (1515–68). He was a brilliant scholar who encouraged the young princess in her learning.

The ordinary people

Most ordinary people in Tudor times lived completely different lives from the luxurious sort enjoyed by the **courtiers** surrounding the king. They lived in small, isolated villages in the countryside, far away from large cities like London. Most worked as farmers or labourers in the fields. Many were very poor and had little to eat. Mothers often died in childbirth and many children died from terrible diseases. It was a difficult time to be poor.

Living in fear

While Henry was married to his last wife, Catherine Parr, Elizabeth and Mary spent more time at the royal court. Catherine was very fond of Elizabeth. The princesses saw more of their little half-brother, Edward, and Elizabeth was with him when their father died in 1547.

The boy king

Edward then **succeeded** his father as Edward VI. He was only nine years old when he became king. Like his half-sister Elizabeth he had been brought up as a **Protestant** and so, for as long as Edward was on the throne, Elizabeth was safe. Unfortunately the new king had always been a sickly child and he died on 6 July 1553, aged fifteen.

A divided kingdom

England was thrown into chaos as Protestants and **Catholics** fought each other for control. Catholic Mary eventually won the support of most of the people of England and was crowned queen. She recognized the Pope as head of the Church in England and restored Catholicism as the state religion. In 1554 she married her Catholic cousin, Prince Philip of Spain.

▶ Edward VI was very well-educated, but he was still a boy when he came to the throne. During his short reign of only six years, England was really ruled by his uncle, the Duke of Somerset.

Princess in the Tower

In February 1554, there was a plot to place Elizabeth on the throne instead of Mary. This was discovered and defeated. Elizabeth was sent to prison in the Tower of London, even though it could not be proved that she had supported the **rebellion**. She remained in prison for three months until she was released in May. But Queen Mary still did not trust her and thought that she was too dangerous to be left alone.

Queen Mary believed she could force the Protestants of England to become Catholic again, and from 1555 nearly 300 Protestants were burned at the stake. Mary was also desperate for a child so that she would be succeeded on the throne by a Catholic. Protestant Elizabeth was still the next in line to be queen. Twice Mary believed that she was pregnant, but she never did have a baby.

▲ Queen Mary was 17 years older than her half-sister Elizabeth. She always felt that it was her duty to reverse many of the changes that their father, King Henry VIII, had introduced.

A Protestant rebellion

In February 1554, a Protestant called Sir Thomas Wyatt led un uprising of 3000 men against Queen Mary. They planned to overthrow Mary and place Elizabeth on the English throne instead. The **rebels** believed that Mary's planned marriage to Prince Philip of Spain would lead to England becoming part of the Catholic Spanish Empire. The rebellion failed and all the leaders were **executed**.

Elizabeth the queen

On 17 November 1558, Mary died and Elizabeth **succeeded** her as Queen of England. Elizabeth was 25 years old. She was crowned queen at Westminster Abbey in London on 15 January 1559. Elizabeth was now the ruler of a country deeply divided between **Catholics** and **Protestants**. Many of the Catholics, especially the Church leaders who had been chosen by Mary, did not recognize Elizabeth as queen. Even the Protestants argued amongst themselves about the sort of Church they wanted.

England in danger

England was also a weak country when Elizabeth came to the throne. It had very little money and it was threatened by much more powerful Catholic countries to the south, especially France and Spain. The fact that Elizabeth was a woman made her position even weaker. This was a time when most rulers were men. Any countries ruled by women were considered to be weak and, therefore, open to attack from abroad and even from inside the country itself.

▲ Hatfield Old Palace in Hertfordshire. Elizabeth was being kept prisoner here when she heard the news that Mary had died and that she was now Queen of England.

A majestic queen

One of Elizabeth's **courtiers** described her in this way: 'Slender and straight; ... her countenance [face] was somewhat long, but yet of admirable beauty, in a most delightful composition of majesty and modesty.'

Elizabeth was about 1.62 m tall and had brown eyes and curly golden red hair with a fair complexion. When she was a princess, she dressed simply with very little jewellery, as she did not want to draw attention to herself. When she became queen she dressed in magnificent clothes made from silks, velvets and furs, and wore fantastic jewels. She dressed to impress her people and foreign **ambassadors**.

▲ This portrait shows Elizabeth in her coronation robes. She is pictured wearing the crown of England on her head and holding the orb and sceptre, symbols of royal power, in her hands.

Clothes for show and for work

The men and women who attended Elizabeth I at her royal court were expected to spend a fortune on their clothes. They were made from the most expensive materials available, like velvet, silk, fur and lace. They were also adorned with beautiful gold jewellery. But most ordinary people in **Tudor** times made their own clothes at home from cotton and wool. Their clothes had to be tough so that they could last a long time.

Loyal advisers

When Elizabeth was growing up, she was never given instruction on how to rule or govern a country. As a girl she was not expected to become ruler of England. But the dangerous times she lived through taught her how to survive and who to trust. When she became Queen of England, Elizabeth liked the taste of power and she made it clear that she would be in charge.

Helpful advice

Elizabeth I was what is known as an absolute ruler. She made all the final decisions on how the country was governed. She could not do everything herself, however, and so she had help from members of her Privy Council. This was a group of men who acted as her advisers.

One of the closest and most important advisers was William Cecil, Lord Burghley. He was Elizabeth's Principal Secretary and he advised her on how to spend the country's money and on England's contacts with other countries. For the next 40 years he would guide the queen through many dangerous situations.

◄ **Lord Burghley (1520–98) rose to become one of the most powerful men in the land and was one of Elizabeth's most respected advisers.**

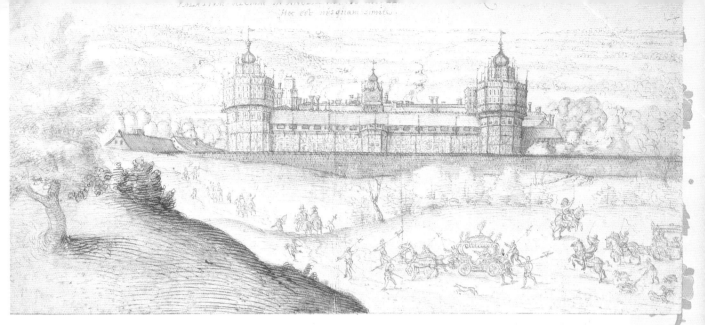

▲ Nonsuch Palace, painted by George Hoefnagel in 1582. Lying to the south-west of London in Surrey, the palace was built by Henry VIII. It was one of Elizabeth's favourite homes and she liked to go hunting in its park.

A new Church

The most important and difficult matter that Elizabeth faced when she came to the throne was that of religion. She made **Protestantism** the official religion of the country. She tried to lead the people of England towards a religion that lay between the beliefs of the **Puritans** on one side, who had been backed by Edward VI, and the **Roman Catholics** on the other, who had been backed by Queen Mary.

Elizabeth hoped that most people in the country would join her Church, so that they could finally settle down and stop fighting each other. Many did, but others refused to recognize her or her Church and so they were hunted down and either **executed** or had to leave the country.

A network of spies

Another of Elizabeth's loyal advisers was called Sir Francis Walsingham (c. 1532–1590). As Secretary of State, he set up a huge network of spies that spread throughout England and across the sea to France, Italy and Spain. Elizabeth always lived in fear of attack. Walsingham's spies sent him information on any planned **rebellions** against the queen. They also protected Elizabeth from plots to kill her.

Married to her country

When Elizabeth became queen, her advisers and all the people of England expected her to marry. In those days they believed that a woman would need the help of a husband to rule the country. They also feared that there would be a **civil war** if Elizabeth did not have a child, who would be the obvious ruler after her death.

During her marriage talks with foreign princes, Elizabeth played one off against the other, holding out the possibility to each of them that they might be able to catch her. In this way, Elizabeth used herself as a source of strength to win more **allies** and power.

A long list of suitors

There were many European princes who were eager to marry the queen. Elizabeth was one of the most desirable women in Europe. One of the first to propose marriage to her was King Philip II of Spain. He had already been married to Elizabeth's half-sister Queen Mary. But he was a **Catholic** and his marriage to Mary had been very unpopular in England. Elizabeth did not want to make the same mistake, so she turned down his offer.

▶ Francis, Duke of Alençon (1554–84). Although he was a Catholic prince, he opposed the strong anti-protestant policies of his brother, King Charles IX of France.

Elizabeth began thinking that it would be safer if she married an Englishman. One man who had known Elizabeth all her life was Robert Dudley, Earl of Leicester. He was already married, however. When his wife was killed falling down some stairs, people began whispering that Robert had had her murdered so that he could marry the queen. These rumours were probably untrue, but they made it impossible for Elizabeth to marry him.

A strong contender

One man who came very close to marrying Elizabeth was Francis, Duke of Alençon. He was the brother of the King of France, but he was another Catholic prince and Elizabeth's advisers thought that it would be too risky to have a Catholic married to their **Protestant** queen. In the end, Elizabeth never married and never had any children. She would later say that she was married to England.

▲ **This painting shows Elizabeth dancing with Robert Dudley, one of her favourite courtiers. She was a very good dancer and musician, and loved to relax in this way with her friends.**

Royal marriages

Royal marriages, like the one between Mary and Philip II of Spain, were extremely important in **Tudor** times. They were regarded as the best way in which to make powerful **alliances** between countries. The rulers of smaller countries would always try to marry their royal children to the sons and daughters of the rulers of more powerful countries. In this way they hoped to strengthen their position and protect themselves from attack by other countries.

A dazzling court

Elizabeth attracted a huge circle of **courtiers** around her. As well as her advisers, there were friends and other people who entertained her. Some hoped to win her favour to help them up the ladder to positions of power. Adventurers and explorers, such as Sir Francis Drake and Sir Walter Raleigh, wanted to win her backing for their **expeditions**. A small army of ladies-in-waiting went everywhere with the queen, looking after her comfort and her magnificent clothes and jewels.

Work and play

Much of Elizabeth's day was spent at her royal duties, meeting her advisers and foreign **ambassadors**. When her working day was over, Elizabeth sat with her friends and ladies-in-waiting to listen to music, dance, play cards and read poetry. She enjoyed watching plays, too, and writers such as Ben Jonson and, later, William Shakespeare wrote plays and poems for her. Artists visited the court to paint magnificent portraits of her. Elizabeth loved sports and was very good at riding, tennis and archery.

▲ The queen was like the sun shining at the centre of her court. Whenever she went out in public, she dazzled everyone who saw her.

▲ This is a modern photograph of Wollaton Hall in Nottinghamshire, which was built in the 1580s by one of Elizabeth's courtiers, Sir Francis Willoughby. The queen often stayed at the houses of her courtiers during her annual 'progress', and she expected to be entertained on a royal scale.

The royal progress

Elizabeth inherited nearly 60 royal residences when she came to the throne. Once a year, during the summer months, Elizabeth and all her **court** would 'progress' from one palace to another. It was very important for Elizabeth to show herself to her people. In this way they were reminded of her presence and power. The queen herself, dressed in splendid clothes, travelled in a coach with open sides so that she could be seen and admired.

Exploring the world

During the 15th and 16th centuries, European seafarers, like Christopher Columbus, began to explore the world. Until then, Europeans knew very little about other countries beyond their shores. In 1577, Sir Francis Drake set out from England and sailed all the way round the world on his ship, the *Golden Hind*. Other English explorers, like Humphrey Gilbert and Sir Walter Raleigh, established settlements in North America.

Royal cousins

In 1568, Elizabeth had to face one of the greatest dangers of her entire reign. In that year her cousin, Queen Mary of Scotland, fled south across the border into England. She had been imprisoned by Scottish **rebels** and forced to give up the Scottish crown to her small son. Only thirteen months old, he now became King James VI of Scotland. Mary begged Elizabeth to help her.

A difficult dilemma

Elizabeth was very suspicious of her cousin. Mary was a **Catholic** and there were many people, both in England and abroad, who believed that she should really be Queen of England instead of Elizabeth. They thought that Henry VIII's marriage to Elizabeth's mother, Anne Boleyn, had not been legal. Mary was allowed to stay in England, but while she lived in great comfort at Elizabeth's expense, she was really under arrest and she was to remain under guard for the next nineteen years.

◀ Mary Queen of Scots was nine years younger than her cousin Elizabeth. She became Queen of Scotland when she was only six days old. Mary was very beautiful, but not a very good ruler.

The kingdom in the north

Scotland had always been a separate kingdom from England. Since 1371 it had been ruled by a royal **dynasty** called the Stuarts. Scotland and England had fought many battles against each other, but there had also been marriage **alliances** between the two countries. King James IV of Scotland married Princess Margaret of England, the sister of Henry VIII. Their granddaughter was Mary Queen of Scots.

Mary is executed

In 1570 the Pope **excommunicated** Elizabeth, giving all English Catholics the right to disobey and rebel against her. A number of plots against Elizabeth were uncovered over the following years and their leaders **executed**. Her advisers warned her that she was in great danger and that Mary must be executed, but she refused to kill her cousin and fellow queen.

Finally, in 1586, it was proved beyond doubt that Mary was plotting against Elizabeth. Letters written to Mary from a young Catholic called Anthony Babington were intercepted by Walsingham's spies. Mary's replies proved that she supported Babington's plan to murder Elizabeth.

Mary was sent for trial and, on 8 February 1587, she was executed. She was 44 years old when she died and had spent nearly half her life as a prisoner of Elizabeth, but the two queens had never met one another.

▲ This 19th century painting shows Mary Queen of Scots being led to her execution at Fotheringay Castle in Northamptonshire. When her son James **succeeded** Elizabeth as King of England, he had the castle pulled down.

Attack from Spain

When Mary Queen of Scots was **executed**, all the ports round England were closed to delay the news reaching Europe. When the **Catholic** rulers of Europe finally heard of her death, they were horrified. King Philip II of Spain now decided that it was his duty to attack Elizabeth and claim the crown of England for himself.

The Spanish Armada

King Philip was a very proud man. He had never forgotten nor forgiven Elizabeth for refusing his offer of marriage. He also knew that she had been sending money and soldiers to help his **Protestant** enemies in his lands in the Netherlands. In 1588, Philip put together an enormous fleet of 130 ships to attack England. It was known as the **Armada**. On 19 July, the fleet was sighted off the south-west coast of England. The Spanish ships sailed up the Channel, followed by the English.

When the Armada anchored off the coast of northern France, the English sent in fire boats to force them out into the open seas. The Spanish sailed out in great confusion and the English gave chase.

The Armada was finally driven north and away from England. Battered by winds and driving rain, the ships were blown all the way round England, Scotland and past Ireland. Many were wrecked along the way. Only half of the original 130 ships made it back to the safety of Spain.

◀ **The Armada Jewel was made for Elizabeth to celebrate the defeat of the Spanish Armada. It is made of gold and brightly coloured enamels, and contains a portrait of the queen.**

Elizabeth's reaction

Before the arrival of the Spanish Armada off the coast of England, Elizabeth travelled to Tilbury on the River Thames. Here she gave a famous speech to inspire her soldiers and sailors. The speech showed Elizabeth as a strong leader, who was not afraid of the Spanish, or anything or anyone else.

▲ This painting shows English ships fighting the Spanish Armada. The Spanish ships were huge, lumbering monsters, much better suited to defending than attacking.

Battleships

England and Spain had about the same number of ships when they fought each other in 1588. But the ships on the two sides were very different. The Spanish ships were enormous and difficult to steer in cramped areas. They carried huge cannons made of brass and iron that fired heavy cannon balls. The English ships were smaller and lighter so they were much quicker and more nimble in the water. They carried much lighter cannons that could be fired more often. Their crews were also more experienced than the Spanish.

The final years

The defeat of the Spanish **Armada** was celebrated throughout the land and Elizabeth I's popularity soared among her people. She came to symbolize the success and glory of her country. England had defeated an attack from the most powerful country in Europe. Now, 30 years after she had first come to the throne, Elizabeth could feel sure of her position as queen of a strong and united **Protestant** country.

The Chancellors Seat

Changing times

As the years passed and Elizabeth grew older, however, things began to change. Even though the Armada had been defeated, the war with Spain continued to drag on. This fighting was very expensive and **taxes** had to be raised in order to pay for the war. Although the people of England still loved their queen, they started to complain about having to pay more and more for the fighting. From 1594 there were four years of bad harvests and many people had little food and were going hungry.

◀ This engraving shows Queen Elizabeth on her throne, with her Privy Counsellors. They were her servants as well as her advisers.

New faces

Elizabeth's close friends and advisers were growing old and dying. One of the first to go was Lord Leicester, who had known Elizabeth since she was a girl. Sir Christopher Hatton, one of her favourite **courtiers** and her **Lord Chancellor**, and the loyal Sir Francis Walsingham died in the next few years. Lord Burghley was growing old and tired.

New men, such as Burghley's son Robert Cecil, were beginning to take over the important positions of power in the land. As Elizabeth's reign drew to a close and the expensive war with Spain dragged on, the members of **Parliament** began to question her authority and her requests for more money. This would have been unimaginable at the beginning of her reign. Elizabeth was beginning to feel isolated and alone.

▲ Robert Cecil, Earl of Salisbury, was the second son of Lord Burghley and **succeeded** his father as chief adviser to Elizabeth and, later, King James VI and I.

God's creation

Europeans in **Tudor** times believed in the idea that God created everything in a strict **hierarchy**, or chain. This was known as the Chain of Being and stretched down from God, through the angels, humans and down to the lowliest things like animals and plants. Some humans, like kings and queens, were seen as higher than others in the chain. **Monarchs** at that time believed that they were appointed by God to rule. This 'divine right of kings' gave them enormous power and influence and their word became law. Parliament was used to pass laws and raise taxes whenever they were demanded by the monarch.

The death of a great queen

As well as losing old friends and advisers, in her old age Elizabeth was losing her looks. She still took immense care over her appearance and wore magnificent clothes and jewels, but her golden red hair was now thin and grey and she wore a wig to cover it up. Her drawn and wrinkled face was covered with white makeup and powder. She became tired very easily and she suffered from painful toothache.

A disloyal courtier

Elizabeth was hit by a bitter blow in her final years. One of her **courtiers**, called the Earl of Essex, returned to England in disgrace after leading a disastrous military **expedition** to Ireland. In desperation and fearing he would be thrown into prison, he tried to raise a **rebellion** against the queen. He was arrested and, in 1601, he was **executed**. Elizabeth was very sorry to sign his **death warrant** as she had known him since he was a boy and had been very fond of him, but she had no choice.

▲ A painting of Queen Elizabeth's funeral procession. Her coffin was drawn through the streets of London, accompanied by some of the most important people in the land.

◀ Queen Elizabeth's tomb at Westminster Abbey. Her successor, King James, erected this large white marble monument to her memory in 1606.

The royal succession

Throughout her long reign, Elizabeth had always refused to name the person she wanted to rule England after her. Now, as that time approached, she still kept everyone guessing to the very end. Early in 1603, Elizabeth caught a chill and moved to her favourite palace at Richmond to recover. By March she had grown so ill that she could eat very little. She grew weaker and weaker and, in the early hours of 24 March 1603, Elizabeth I, the last of the **Tudors**, died peacefully in her sleep. She was 69 and had reigned for 44 years.

A messenger was sent from Richmond to carry the news to King James VI of Scotland. The son of Elizabeth's cousin and old enemy, Mary Queen of Scots, had now become James I of England.

London in Elizabeth's time

By the time of Elizabeth's death in 1603, London had grown into one of the largest and most important cities in Europe. Many thousands of people lived there. Rich nobles and **merchants** lived in grand mansions, but most people were packed into tall, narrow houses and lived in cramp conditions. There was a busy port and ships sailed up and down the River Thames, which ran through the middle of the city.

The end of a golden age

Elizabeth I's body was taken from Richmond by boat to her palace in Whitehall, London. Her funeral was held in Westminster Abbey at the end of April, and as the **procession** wound its way through the streets of London there was 'a general sighing, groaning and weeping' among the crowds that lined the streets. Elizabeth I was buried in a magnificent tomb next to that of her half-sister, Mary. In another chamber nearby lies the body of Mary Queen of Scots. In death, Elizabeth was finally united with the two Marys who had played such an important part in her life.

England mourns

Many people throughout England **mourned** Elizabeth's death. They saw her long reign as a golden age in England's history. They forgot about how difficult their lives had been in the final years, the shortages of food and the constant demands for money to pay for expensive wars. They preferred to remember Elizabeth as a wise and loving queen who protected her country and her people from many threats and dangers.

▶ This miniature portrait of Queen Elizabeth by the famous artist Nicholas Hilliard is shown here bigger than it really is. Even in old age, the queen was still portayed in splendid clothes and jewels.

Elizabeth did make mistakes, especially at the start of her reign. She had received no training in how to govern a country and she was given bad advice by some of her advisers. After these early mistakes Elizabeth made it clear that she would be the one in charge. She often found it difficult to make up her mind on important matters. Once she did, however, she did it with a determination and certainty that impressed her friends and her enemies, too.

◄ This is a portrait of King James VI of Scotland, James I of England. As soon as he was told of Elizabeth's death, he hurried south to London to claim his new throne.

A sense of pride

When Elizabeth died, she left England a proud, confident and strong nation. She united her people under the **Protestant** faith and they looked out as equal partners with the other nations of Europe. Her reign is of such importance in the history of England that she was the first English ruler to give her name to an age. The Elizabethan age was truly a golden era.

Glossary

alliance being united, through a formal treaty or an agreement, such as a marriage

allies two or more people or countries united by some formal agreement

ambassador person who represents the interests of their own country in another country

Armada large number of ships, from the Spanish word for 'great fleet'

astronomy scientific study of the stars and planets

Catholic member of the Christian Roman Catholic Church, headed by the Pope in Rome

civil war war fought between two sides within the same country

court home of a king and queen and their household and followers

courtier attendant at a royal court

death warrant document that, when signed, allows someone to be put to death

dynasty series of rulers belonging to the same family

excommunicate cast someone out of membership of the Church, particularly the Catholic Church

execute put someone to death

expedition organized journey or voyage, for exploration, military or scientific purposes

hierarchy system of arranging people or things in a graded order, from top to bottom

illegitimate someone who was born when their parents were not legally married to each other

inherit receive property or a title from someone who has died

Lord Chancellor chief adviser to the English monarch

merchant someone who trades with other countries, buying and selling different goods

monarch king, queen, emperor or empress who rules a country

mourn to express sadness at the death or loss of someone

Parliament body that passes the laws of the land and raises taxes. In Elizabeth I's time, Parliament had less power than it does today.

procession group of people moving forward in an organized, ceremonial way

Protestant member of the Protestant branch of the Christian Church, which broke away from the Catholic Church, headed by the Pope

Puritan extreme Protestant who wants to purify the Church of England

rebel someone who resists or rises up against a government or ruler

rebellion organized resistance to a government or ruler

succeed to follow as the new king or queen

taxes money that individuals have to pay to the government

Tudor royal dynasty that ruled England from 1485 until 1603

virginals early form of the piano, in which the strings are plucked rather than struck

Timeline

1509   Henry VIII becomes King of England. Henry marries Princess Catherine of Aragon.

1516   Princess Mary is born

1517   The beginning of the Reformation in Europe (Protestantism)

1533   Henry divorces Catherine of Aragon and marries Anne Boleyn. Princess Elizabeth is born.

1534   Henry declares himself head of the Church in England

1536   Queen Anne Boleyn is executed. Henry marries Jane Seymour.

1537   Prince Edward is born

1542   Princess Mary of Scotland is born. She becomes queen six days later when her father, James V, dies.

1547   Edward becomes King of England when Henry VIII dies

1553   Edward VI dies and is succeeded by his half-sister Mary

1558   Mary I dies and Elizabeth I succeeds her

1568   Mary Queen of Scots escapes to England

1570   Pope excommunicates Elizabeth I

1587   Mary Queen of Scots is executed

1588   The Spanish Armada is defeated

1603   Elizabeth I dies and James VI (James I) becomes King of England as well as King of Scotland

Further reading & websites

Investigating the Tudors, A. Honey (National Trust, 1993)

Queen Elizabeth I, R. Bell (Heinemann Library, 1999)

Queen Elizabeth I, P. Burns (Wayland, 1999)

Heinemann Explore – an online resource from Heinemann. For Key Stage 2 history go to *www.heinemannexplore.co.uk*

www.elizabethi.org/

http://tudorhistory.org/elizabeth/

Places to visit

Hatfield House, Hertfordshire   Burghley House, Northamptonshire

Westminster Abbey, London   Tower of London

Index